MODERN STARS

ARIANA GRANDE

by Sue Bradford Edwards

Essential Library
An Imprint of Abdo Publishing
abdobooks.com

ABDOBOOKS.COM

Published by Abdo Publishing, a division of ABDO, PO Box 398166, Minneapolis, Minnesota 55439.

Printed in China.
102025
012026

Cover Photo: David Swanson/AFP/Getty Images
Interior Photos: Patrick T. Fallon/AFP/Getty Images, 5; Rich Polk/Penske Media/Getty Images, 7; Kevin Winter/Getty Images Entertainment/Getty Images, 9, 37; Kevin Mazur/Getty Images for Ariana Grande/Getty Images Entertainment/Getty Images, 10, 71, 75, 76; Valerie Macon/AFP/Getty Images, 13; Silver Screen Collection/Moviepix/Getty Images, 15; Jim Spellman/WireImage/Getty Images, 16; Jeff Kravitz/FilmMagic, Inc/Getty Images, 19; Alberto E. Rodriguez/Getty Images Entertainment/Getty Images, 23; Bruce Glikas/FilmMagic/Getty Images, 25, 31; Earl Gibson III/WireImage/Getty Images, 26; John Barrett/Globe Photos/ZUMA Press, Inc./Alamy, 29; Frederic J. Brown/AFP/Getty Images, 33; Chelsea Lauren/WireImage/Getty Images, 34, 38; Brill/ullstein bild/Getty Images, 41; Larry Busacca/Getty Images Entertainment/Getty Images, 45; Richard Milnes/Alamy Live News/Alamy, 47; Universal Pictures Television/Warner Bros./Album/Alamy, 48; Ben Stansall/AFP/Getty Images, 51; Dave Hogan for One Love Manchester/Getty Images Entertainment/Getty Images, 52; Kevin Mazur/Getty Images for March For Our Lives/Getty Images Entertainment/Getty Images, 55; Christopher Polk/Getty Images Entertainment/Getty Images, 56; Mike Coppola/MTV1617/Getty Images for MTV/Getty Images for Entertainment/Getty Images, 58; Kevin Mazur/WireImage/Getty Images, 61; Kevin Mazur/Getty Images for American Express/Getty Images Entertainment/Getty Images, 62; Kevin Winter/Getty Images for iHeartMedia/Getty Images Entertainment/Getty Images, 65; Shutterstock Images, 68; Kevin Mazur/Getty Images for Coachella/Getty Images Entertainment/Getty Images, 72; Hyperobject Industries/Album/Alamy, 81; Kevin Mazur/Getty Images for iHeartMedia/Getty Images Entertainment/Getty Images, 83; John Shearer/97th Oscars/The Academy/Getty Images Entertainment/Getty Images, 85; Dimitrios Kambouris/MG18/Getty Images for The Met Museum/Vogue/Getty Images Entertainment/Getty Images, 87; Kevin Mazur/MG24/Getty Images for The Met Museum/Vogue/Getty Images Entertainment/Getty Images, 90; BFA/Universal Pictures/Alamy, 93; FlixPix/Universal Pictures/Alamy, 96, 98

Editor: Kari Cornell
Series Designer: Karli Hughes

Library of Congress Control Number: 2025939298

PUBLISHER'S CATALOGING-IN-PUBLICATION DATA

Names: Edwards, Sue Bradford, author.
Title: Ariana Grande / by Sue Bradford Edwards
Description: Minneapolis, Minnesota: Abdo Publishing, 2026 | Series: Modern stars | Includes online resources and index.
Identifiers: ISBN 9781098298081 (lib. bdg.) | ISBN 9798384931881 (ebook)
Subjects: LCSH: Grande, Ariana--Juvenile literature. | Singers--United States--Biography--Juvenile literature. | Motion picture actors and actresses--United States--Biography--Juvenile literature. | Businesspeople--Biography--Juvenile literature.
Classification: DDC 782.42166--dc23

CONTENTS

Chapter 1
LIVE! 4

Chapter 2
CHILDHOOD YEARS 12

Chapter 3
BUILDING A MUSIC CAREER 22

Chapter 4
AWARD WINNER 32

Chapter 5
A LITTLE MOONLIGHT 44

Chapter 6
SWEETENER 54

Chapter 7
HER OWN RULES 64

Chapter 8
POSITIONS 74

Chapter 9
THE MET AND MORE 84

Chapter 10
THE BIG SCREEN 92

Essential Facts 100
Glossary 102
Additional Resources 104
Source Notes 106
Index 110
About the Author 112

CHAPTER ONE

LIVE!

On Sunday, March 2, 2025, the Academy of Motion Picture Arts and Sciences gathered for the 97th Academy Awards ceremony. During this event, the Academy handed out the awards known as the Oscars. The event began with a video montage called "The Oscars Love LA."

The video opened with a clip from the 1939 movie *The Wizard of Oz*, in which Judy Garland, playing Dorothy Gale, says, "There's no place like home." On the screen, Garland clicked together the heels of her ruby slippers. But instead of continuing the scene from *The Wizard of Oz*, a view of Los Angeles, California, the home of the Academy, appeared on the screen.

The montage paid homage to the city's rich history of moviemaking. The video featured scenes from famous films set in Los Angeles, including *Barbie*,

Grande wore a red strapless ball gown designed by Maison Schiaparelli when she performed at the 2025 Academy Awards. >>

Iron Man 2, and *La La Land*. It closed with a view of the night sky in which sparkling lights formed a big red heart.

The stage darkened and the orchestra began to play a familiar tune. Ariana Grande launched into singing "Somewhere over the Rainbow" from *The Wizard of Oz*. This iconic movie stars Garland as a girl whose house has been swept up by a tornado and dropped into a magical land.

The film is a fantasy musical adaptation of the novel *The Wonderful Wizard of Oz*, published in 1900 by L. Frank Baum. Grande's sparkling red gown shimmered as the lights came up and the iridescent colors of a rainbow surrounded her. The audience applauded enthusiastically as Grande finished the song and exited the stage.

ON *THE WIZARD OF OZ* AND JUDY GARLAND

"I have always been a big fan of *The Wizard of Oz* since I was a little girl," Grande said in an interview. She explained that she thought the story had broad appeal because of its themes of being lost or rejected and seeking friends. Grande admitted that she had a favorite dress like the one Dorothy wore in the movie and that she watched the movie to carefully study Judy Garland. She explained, "I would pay attention to how she sang and the way she moved her arms."[1]

Grande's costar in the Oscar-nominated movie *Wicked*, Cynthia Erivo, entered the stage wearing a white gown

Grande and her *Wicked* costar Cynthia Erivo met for the first time when they started working on the movie. The two connected instantly.

adorned with purple flowers. She sang "Home" from *The Wiz*, a 1974 Broadway musical adaptation of *The Wizard of Oz* that reimagined the story in Harlem, a neighborhood in New York City. The audience again applauded and cheered as Erivo finished.

As Erivo began to sing "Defying Gravity," the song that is the climax of *Wicked*, Grande joined her onstage. Their film was based on the 2003 Broadway musical *Wicked*, which in turn was adapted from the 1995 Gregory Maguire novel about Elphaba, the wicked witch from *The Wizard of Oz*. The new *Wicked* film had received ten award nominations, including Best Actress in a Leading Role for Erivo's performance as Elphaba and Best Actress in a Supporting Role for Grande's role as Galinda.[2]

ON THE MEDLEY

Critics had a lot to say about the Oscar performances of Grande and Erivo. Melissa Ruggieri is the national music writer for *USA Today.* In her review of the event, she wrote, "Not only did Ariana Grande and Cynthia Erivo defy gravity during their spectacular opening performance, but defied every conceivable expectation."[3] She then went on to describe Grande's performance in "Somewhere over the Rainbow" as filled with vocal curlicues, an apt description of the spiraling notes. She explained that in "Defying Gravity," Erivo nailed the finale, hitting the astonishing high note at the end before everyone leaped to their feet to praise the two singers.

Grande kissed the back of Erivo's hand and then backed away from center stage to leave her costar as the focus of the finale. As the two finished singing, a red heart like the one in the "Oscars Love LA" video appeared behind them, the orchestra played its final chord, and the audience rose to their feet, cheering and applauding.

After thanking the audience, Grande and Erivo left the stage to take their seats among the audience. Later in the evening, Da'Vine Joy Randolph, who had won the award for Best Actress in a Supporting Role in 2024, took the stage to read the names of the 2025 nominees in the category. She named each actress who had been nominated, saying something about her value and skill as a performer.

"Ariana, your joy, your love is infectious. It is your voice, it is in your movement, your presence. You light up every

Da'Vine Joy Randolph announced the 2025 Best Actress in a Supporting Role nominees. They were Monica Barbaro, Ariana Grande, Felicity Jones, Isabella Rossellini, and Zoe Saldaña.

single screen the same way you light up the stage. You are pure magic," she said when she introduced Grande.[4]

Cameras were focused on all five of the nominees as Randolph opened the envelope and announced the winner. "And the Oscar goes to Zoe Saldaña."[5] Grande rose with the others, smiling and clapping for Saldaña. The nomination showed that Grande's talent and star power extended to the world of movies.

WHO IS ARIANA GRANDE?

Ariana Grande was nominated for an Oscar for her acting performance, but she is best known as a singer

Grande performed with Mikey Foster of Social House in London, England, during her Sweetener World Tour.

and songwriter. Part of the reason for her fame is her impressive vocal range. Grande's voice spans a four-octave range, allowing her to hit not only high notes other people can reach only by whistling but also low notes with the strength needed to sing popular Broadway songs. Julianne Escobedo Shepherd of *Billboard* compared Grande to legendary singer Mariah Carey. Grande credits Carey and acclaimed performer Whitney Houston as being her inspirations.

"I love Mariah Carey. She is literally my favorite human being on the planet. And of course Whitney as well. As far as vocal influences go, Whitney and Mariah pretty much cover it."[6]

—Ariana Grande, January 2012 *Limelight* interview

Grande has drawn fans not just with her technical singing skills but also with how she expresses herself musically. In a review of Grande's 2018 album *Sweetener*, Jon Pareles, a pop music critic for the *New York Times*, says that while Grande has taken a lot of inspiration from singers such as Carey, her voice is unmistakable. "It can be silky, breathy or cutting, swooping through long melismas or jabbing out short R&B phrases; it's always supple and airborne, never forced. With *Sweetener*, she has reaffirmed that the lightness of her voice is best suited for bliss and satisfaction, not mourning."[7]

Grande's music has been described as pop or rhythm and blues, also known as R&B. She sings music that she writes herself as well as music written for her by others. She often performs with other musicians, and these collaborations help push her career forward. Grande is a versatile artist with a love of performing that began when she was less than ten years old.

GRANDE'S RANGE

American Standard Pitch Notation (ASPN) is a way of writing out musical notes that combines the note (A through G) with the octave number. There are ten octaves, and each octave contains eight notes. When written in ASPN, Ariana Grande's vocal range is D3 to E7. This means that the lowest note she can sing is D in the third octave, and her highest note is E in the seventh octave. This range makes her a soprano, the highest of the four vocal ranges—soprano, alto, tenor, and bass. Knowing her range helps Grande pick out music that complements her voice.

CHAPTER TWO

CHILDHOOD YEARS

Ariana Grande-Butera was born on June 26, 1993, in Boca Raton, Florida. Her mother, Joan Grande, is the chief executive officer (CEO) of Hose-McCann Communications in Deerfield Beach, Florida. This family-owned business manufactures communications and safety equipment.

Her father, Edward Butera, owns a graphic design firm in Boca Raton. Both of her parents are Italian Americans, and they moved along with her older half-brother, Frankie Grande, from New York to Florida shortly before Ariana was born. Another close family member is her maternal grandmother, Marjorie Grande.

Ariana attended the 2020 Grammy Awards with her parents, Joan Grande and Edward Butera. >>

62
ARIANA
GRANDE
TALENT

GLORIA ESTEFAN

Famed singer Gloria Estefan heard four-year-old Ariana sing. Ariana was on a cruise with her family but didn't want to participate in the children's activities. Instead, she went to karaoke. The song she chose was "My Heart Will Go On" from the movie *Titanic*. After she sang, a stranger who was also on a family vacation spoke to Ariana and her mother. That stranger was Estefan, and she encouraged Ariana to keep singing.

As a child, Ariana attended Pine Crest School and North Broward Preparatory. She was interested in music and theater at a young age. She sang the national anthem at a Florida Panthers National Hockey League (NHL) game in 2002, when she was eight years old. That was also the year Ariana performed at the Little Palm Family Theatre, where she played the title role in *Annie*.

She began to sing with different orchestras on cruise ships that sailed around South Florida during this time as well. When Ariana was eight, her parents divorced. She continued to perform with the Little Palm Family Theatre, and as a ten-year-old, Ariana starred in the theater's production of *The Wizard of Oz*, performed at the Crest Theater in Delray Beach, Florida.

MUSICAL INFLUENCES

Even as a child, Ariana was a music fan. She listened to a variety of music at home and attended concerts with

Judy Garland starred as Dorothy, *center*, in *The Wizard of Oz*, which was released in 1939.

her mother. When the pop band NSYNC returned to their home state of Florida to film a TV special, six-year-old Ariana was caught on film in her mother's arms, singing along to the song. Ariana's mother shared her love of music with her daughter whenever she could.

As an adult, Ariana still lists actress Judy Garland, who sang and acted in movies from 1936 through 1969, as one of her musical influences. She and her mother watched Garland on video every day, selecting a different concert or movie. Ariana loved that Garland used her voice to

The Broadway musical *13* opened at the Bernard B. Jacobs Theatre in October 2008 and closed in early January 2009.

tell a story through song without needing elaborate hair or costumes.

Another inspiration for Ariana was Whitney Houston. When Ariana and her mother watched *The Bodyguard*, a 1992 film in which Houston plays a celebrity singer, Ariana would listen to Houston sing and then tell her mother that she wanted to perform like that one day. "Her riffs are so precise, and I love her tone," Ariana explained.[1]

At the age of 15, Ariana traveled to New York to audition for the 2008 Broadway musical *13*. The play tells the story of 13-year-old Evan's move to a small Indiana town from New York City after his parents' divorce. Evan struggles to fit in at his new school and prepare for his upcoming Bar Mitzvah.

KIDS WHO CARE

At ten, Ariana was one of the founding members of the group Kids Who Care, a children's troupe that formed after the Little Palm Family Theatre closed. The group consisted of young singers including Ariana, Misha Lambert, and Aaron Simon Gross. They performed Broadway songs at charity events and senior homes. In 2007, the group raised more than $500,000 for various local charities.[3]

Jason Robert Brown, who composed the music for *13*, was impressed with Ariana's talents. He said, "She sang Mariah Carey. She opened her mouth, and we said, 'We have to cast her.'"[2] Ariana was cast as Charlotte, one of the cheerleaders, and was an understudy for the leading role of Patrice. The musical ran for only a few months, but that was enough time for her to attract the attention of Nickelodeon, a television network specializing in programs for kids.

VICTORIOUS

Ariana and her *13* costar Elizabeth Gillies auditioned in New York for a new Nickelodeon series called *Victorious*. The series was about a group of students at Hollywood Arts, a fictional performing arts high school. Ariana was cast in the role of Cat Valentine, and Gillies played Jade West, the lead character.

Victorious was a joint production between Nickelodeon and the Columbia/Epic Label Group of Sony Music Entertainment. At the time, mixing television shows with musical elements was popular in the industry. Walt Disney Company had the *Hannah Montana* franchise, built around teen singer Miley Cyrus. The Fox show *Glee* had expanded to include live performances and albums. Nickelodeon wanted to create something similar.

"What we really do best is to follow where kids are. Kids are into music, maybe more than ever," said Nickelodeon executive Marjorie Cohn.[4] *Victorious* would

Ariana, *second from right*, attended the TeenNick HALO Awards In October 2011 with cast members from *Victorious*.

feature song-and-dance productions several times each season. Original music was written for the series.

Victorious premiered on March 27, 2010, after the network's popular *Kids' Choice Awards*. Placing the new show after the major event worked, with 76 percent of the kids who watched the awards program continuing to watch *Victorious*. It was one of the biggest premieres in Nickelodeon's history, drawing 5.7 million viewers.[5]

Ariana was asked to dye her naturally dark hair red for the part of Cat Valentine. Nickelodeon didn't want all actresses in *Victorious* to have dark hair. This meant recoloring her hair red every other week, as it grew out and her dark natural color showed at the roots. This ultimately left it damaged.

TALENT MANAGERS

Most musicians have managers who handle business matters to allow the artists to focus on their art. This includes helping determine which opportunities will move an artist's career forward. Managers don't always agree with the artist about what that next step should be. In an interview with *Billboard*, Grande talked about meeting with her managers in Los Angeles. When she told them she wanted to make an R&B-style album, they told her the goal was ambitious and that no one would buy such a record from a 14-year-old singer.

Ariana's first opportunity to sing on *Victorious* came when she performed "Give It Up" with Gillies. The song appeared in the season-one episode "Freak the Freak Out," when Cat and Jade are challenged to sing in a karaoke contest. The song was later featured on the album *Victorious: Music from the Hit TV Show*, which was released in August 2011. Ariana sang another song in season four that ended up on the third *Victorious* album.

Ariana sang many songs as Cat Valentine that didn't appear on the albums. In a season-one episode called "The Diddley-Bops," Cat and her fellow students perform at a kids' party when the original entertainment, a musical group called the Waggafuffles, is in an accident. Cat sings "The Waggafuffles Song," a song by this fictional group.

Cat and the other students call themselves the Diddley-Bops and sing "Favorite Food" with Cat dressed as broccoli.

> **"When I was younger, people loved Cat so much I used to pretend to be more like her. It took me a long time to be brave enough to separate myself."**[7]
>
> **—Ariana Grande on Cat Valentine, July 2014**

Not every song was original. In season two, Ariana and the cast sang the Jackson 5 song "I Want You Back" in the hour-long special episode "Locked Up." In season three, episode seven, "Tori and Jade's Play Date," the cast rapped "Five Fingaz to the Face," which had originally been performed by Dr. Rhapsody.

When *Victorious* was canceled, Ariana decided to concentrate on her music. She had enjoyed working on the TV series with her friends, but it wasn't what she wanted to focus on. "Music has always been first and foremost with me," said Grande.[6]

CHAPTER THREE

BUILDING A MUSIC CAREER

While working on *Victorious*, Grande would record videos of herself singing covers of songs by Adele, Whitney Houston, and Mariah Carey, which she uploaded to YouTube. Her online presence and her role on *Victorious* helped her gather a loyal fan base that came to be known as Ariana's Army but is now called the Arianators. Through social media, more people became aware of Grande's talent.

One of these people was a friend of Monte Lipman, CEO of Republic Records, a division of Universal Music Group. When Lipman viewed her videos, he liked what he heard. He met with Grande, and she signed a recording contract with Republic in August 2011.

By 2011, Grande was ready to focus on her music career. >>

To help Grande create her first album, Republic contacted Matt Squire, a songwriter who specializes in helping up-and-coming artists create their identities. Squire wasn't accustomed to working with someone like Grande. She already had a strong fan base and three million followers on Twitter, the platform now known as X. But Republic wanted Grande to create a musical identity and move beyond her role as Cat from *Victorious*. The music they created for this album would shape this new persona.

By the time Squire met with Grande, he had a variety of samples prepared. Grande told him he would probably be surprised by the music she was interested in making. She selected "Put Your Hearts Up," an interpolation of "What's Up," a song by 4 Non-Blondes. Linda Perry of

PINK CHAMPAGNE

One of the earliest songs that Matt Squire and Ariana Grande worked on together was "Pink Champagne." Cowritten by singer-songwriter Kesha, it was recorded but never released for sale. As with "Put Your Hearts Up," the song simply didn't match the sound and personality Grande wanted on her first album, *Yours Truly*. Grande sometimes posts unreleased music on social media. In October 2013, she released "Pink Champagne" online to celebrate reaching ten million Twitter followers.[1]

Grande promoted her "Put Your Hearts Up" CD release at the Planet Hollywood restaurant in Times Square, New York, in December 2011.

4 Non-Blondes granted permission for Grande to adapt the song.

Squire had expected her to choose an original song, not an interpolation. "Put Your Hearts Up" has been called bubblegum pop, a term used to describe music with a catchy tune and simple lyrics. It was a piece Grande had chosen as a tribute to her fans, who often made heart-shaped gestures with their hands during her Listening Sessions concert tour in August 2013. The tour promoted the songs that would appear on her debut album.

Squire and Grande continued to work on songs for the upcoming album. The rest of the songs were more in the

Grande took the stage as Snow White at the Pasadena Playhouse when she was 19 years old.

styles of Motown or doo-wop, which both sound quite different from "Put Your Hearts Up." Because of this, they decided to release "Put Your Hearts Up" on December 12, 2011, as her first single instead of saving it for the album. It sold more than 500,000 copies in the United States, which means it was certified Gold by the Recording Industry Association of America (RIAA).[2]

OTHER PROJECTS

While working on the music for her first album, Grande was involved in many other projects. In December 2012 she collaborated on the single "Popular Song," a duet with British singer and songwriter Mika for his third album, *The Origin of Love*. Mika's song is based on "Popular," a song sung by Galinda in *Wicked*. The song was released on December 21 and peaked at No. 87 on the *Billboard* Hot 100 chart.

In December 2012, Grande also starred as Snow White in *A Snow White Christmas*. The Pasadena Playhouse production was a panto-style play, which is a form of British family-friendly theater that is interactive and humorous. The play ran from December 13 to 30.

In 2013, Grande performed in a Nickelodeon adaptation of the 2008 book *Swindle* by Gordon Korman. In the movie, a character finds an old baseball card, which a friend persuades him to sell. When he sells the card, the buyer refuses to give him the full value, swindling him out of more than $1 million. His friend assembles a team of teens to help him get the card back. Grande plays gymnast Amanda Benson, who is selected to help with the heist specifically for her acrobatic abilities.

That year, Grande also starred in a *Victorious* spin-off series, *Sam & Cat*. Grande and her *Victorious* costar Jennette McCurdy play their characters from the show, Cat Valentine and Sam Puckett, in this buddy sitcom about two girls who are roommates and have an after-school babysitting business. The show ran for only one season, but Grande was already hard at work on her music career under the direction of manager Scooter Braun, who also worked with Justin Bieber.

YOURS TRULY

For Grande, the big news for 2013 was the release of her first album, *Yours Truly*. Several singles paved the way to the full album release. "The Way," featuring rapper Mac Miller, dropped on March 26. The song topped the sales chart within hours. It also debuted on the *Billboard* Hot 100 at No. 10, becoming the first top-ten hit for either artist.

Grande and Miller didn't have a budget when they decided to shoot the video for this R&B song. "We said, 'Listen, we have a camera, we have a projector, we have music, we have balloons, we got dancers,'" Grande tweeted to her fans.[3] Later, when Republic told her they needed to

"TROGLODYTE" LAWSUIT

Grande's song "The Way" begins with the spoken line, "What we gotta do right here is go back. Back to the top." These words were all it took to launch a lawsuit in December 2013. Minder Music owns the rights to songs written and performed by the 1970s funk group the Jimmy Castor Bunch. The group's 1972 song "Troglodyte" opens with a similar spoken-word line: "What we're gonna do right here is go back, way back, back into time."[4] The words aren't identical, but a lawsuit by Minder Music claimed that the cadence and pacing are. The suit was settled out of court for an undisclosed amount.

Grande and Mac Miller performed their song "The Way" on the *Today Show* in September 2013.

shoot a video, she gave them what she and Miller had already produced. It was released on March 28, and fans saw a dark-haired singer who resembled Cat Valentine but had a persona that was completely different. This was the more mature Ariana Grande.

The second single, "Baby I," released on July 22. With this song, some reviewers compared Grande to Mariah Carey. This was because both singers have a wide vocal range and an ability to hit high notes. "Baby I" debuted at No. 21 on the *Billboard* Hot 100. The song is about not being able to express feelings. Grande told MTV that she is often flustered when trying to express herself around new people.

The final single, "Right There," came out on August 6. The song, a collaboration with rapper Big Sean, debuted at No. 84 on the *Billboard* Hot 100. Grande said she considered the song a sequel to "The Way." Unlike "The

Way," the video for "Right There" features Grande as the character of Juliet from Shakespeare's *Romeo and Juliet* at a lavish Halloween masked ball.

Yours Truly was released on August 30. Reviewers described the musical influences for the album as doo-wop, 1990s hip-hop and R&B, dance-pop, and musical theater. Two of the songs Grande had worked on with Squire made it onto the album, "Tattooed Heart" and "Honeymoon Avenue," which was the first track.

The album went above and beyond the 120,000 copies Republic hoped would sell in the first week. The 138,000 copies sold meant the album debuted at the top of the *Billboard* 200 chart of top-selling albums.[5] Grande became the fifteenth female artist to reach the top of the list with her first album.

Before her album was even released, Grande was preparing to go on her mini-tour. This meant working out at the gym to build up her lung capacity to support her voice, but

A CHRISTMAS ALBUM

After releasing *Yours Truly*, Grande began to record holiday tracks. Starting on November 19, Grande released a Christmas song each week for four weeks. The songs were then sold together as an extended play (EP) album called *Christmas Kisses*. The EP included two classic holiday songs, "Last Christmas" by Wham! and "Santa Baby" by Eartha Kitt. Grande also performed two original songs, "Love Is Everything" and "Snow in California."

she also had to train her voice. This included learning how to keep muscles relaxed and how to breathe properly. Voice training produces a better sound and helps singers avoid straining their voice.

She joined pop star Justin Bieber for three August shows during his Believe Tour. Then she launched her own mini-tour, The Listening Sessions. She played nine cities between August 13 and August 31, beginning in Silver Spring, Maryland, and finishing in Kansas City, Missouri.

> **"I just wanted it to be sort of a love letter, an introduction to the world, and how you sign a letter . . . is 'yours truly.'"**[6]
>
> **—Ariana Grande on naming *Yours Truly***

On November 24, 2013, Grande performed "The Way" at the American Music Awards (AMAs). She ended the song with a vocal riff and then launched into "Tattooed Heart." Before the ceremony was over, Grande had been named the New Artist of the Year for her work in 2013. She was new, but she was already making a name for herself in the world of music.

During her Listening Sessions Tour, Grande played 11 shows across North America.

CHAPTER FOUR

AWARD WINNER

For Grande, 2014 got off to a great start. On January 8, she received the People's Choice Award for Favorite Breakout Artist for 2014. These awards are run by the E! cable network. Fans vote online for their favorite singers, movies, and more. Grande proved once again that she has a strong fan base.

On March 6, Grande sang at the White House. She was part of "Women of Soul: In Performance at the White House," a concert organized by First Lady Michelle Obama. Grande was one of seven women, including Aretha Franklin, Patti LaBelle, and Melissa Etheridge, who sang blues, jazz, soul, R&B, and rock and roll.

Obama chose some of the performers based on their impact on music culture in the United States. Others were newcomers whose work deals with the

In 2014, Grande performed at the MTV Video Music Awards and won Best Pop Video for "Problem," which featured singer Iggy Azalea. >>

Grande performed with Big Sean at the StubHub Center in Los Angeles in May 2014.

struggles of women. Grande performed both "Tattooed Heart" from her first album and the Whitney Houston song "I Have Nothing." The concert was performed in front of an audience that included President Barack Obama, and it was streamed live from the White House.

On April 21, Grande returned to the White House to perform at the annual Easter Egg Roll. Wearing a light purple sweater and white go-go boots, Grande sang "Right There" with Big Sean. Other entertainers at the event included the cast of the children's show *Sesame Street* and actor Jim Carrey, who Grande revealed was a childhood favorite. Grande took the time to pose for selfies and sign autographs for fans.

COLLABORATIONS

Grande had begun work on her next album shortly after the release of *Yours Truly*. One of the first songs she tackled was "Problem," but she didn't think it was strong enough to include on the album. She invited Australian rapper Iggy Azalea to work with her on it. Grande and Azalea teamed up with a few songwriters to finalize the song, which is about deciding whether to get back together with an ex.

When the time came to record, the producers Max Martin, Savan Kotecha, and Ilya Salmanzadeh decided Grande should begin with a spoken-word phrase. They thought this would sound sexy, but it came off as creepy instead. Everyone in the studio started laughing about how creepy it sounded.

Grande's laughter was recorded, and this is how they decided to begin the song, which was released on April 28. The music video came out the next day.

PUBLIC PERCEPTION

Grande has admitted that initially her onstage style duplicated the iconic style of 1950s actress Audrey Hepburn, but in 2014 she decided that it was time to start dressing like a young woman and not a teen idol. "On stage I love a very 60s go-go kinda look," Grande told *Grazia* magazine.[1] That meant a change to short skirts and knee-high boots when performing, a look that many publications commented on.

"Problem" quickly climbed to No. 2 on the *Billboard* 100 chart in the United States. The single sold 438,000 copies in its first week, making the 20-year-old Grande the youngest woman to debut with more than 400,000 copies sold in the first week.[2]

The second single from the album was "Break Free," which featured Russian-German producer and musician Zedd. The song, which was released on July 2 with the video following in August, reached No. 4 on the *Billboard* Hot 100 chart. In the video, Grande wears a costume inspired by actress Jane Fonda's look in the 1968 sci-fi film *Barbarella*. The video features Grande on an alien world where she frees a group of captives before they all leave in her spaceship.

In another collaboration, Grande and rapper Nicki Minaj came together with singer Jessie J to work on "Bang Bang." The same trio of producers who worked on "Problem" worked on this song. Each of the performers sang a verse, and the song was released on July 29 as the lead single for Jessie J's third album, *Sweet Talker*. Grande also included the song as the third single from her own upcoming album.

The song hit No. 3 on the *Billboard* Hot 100 chart in the United States. Its success meant Grande had three

Grande and Zedd performed their song "Break Free" at the iHeartRadio Festival in Las Vegas, Nevada, in 2016.

songs in the top ten at one time, making her one of just four artists to have achieved this status. On May 23, the RIAA announced that the song had achieved Diamond status, meaning more than ten million copies had been sold or downloaded. This was the first time an all-female collaboration had achieved this status. It was a second Diamond status for Minaj and the first for Grande.

THE ALBUM

Grande's second studio album, *My Everything*, was released in August 2014. It debuted in the top ten of the *Billboard* 200 with 169,000 copies sold or downloaded.[3] *Rolling Stone* magazine praised the

Grande and The Weeknd took the stage during KIIS FM's Jingle Ball in Los Angeles to perform "Love Me Harder" and other songs.

album, stating, "It's a confident, intelligent, brazen pop statement, mixing bubblegum diva vocals with EDM break beats."[4] The magazine emphasized that "Break Free" set the tone for the entire album, although it was critical of the songs featuring rappers Iggy Azalea and Big Sean.

Rolling Stone praised "Bang Bang" as a "perfect Max Martin throwdown."[5] Max Martin was the Swedish producer who worked on the single. "Bang Bang" was featured as a bonus track available only on the deluxe edition of *My Everything*. A review in the *Los Angeles Times* said that this marked Grande's ascent to the top ranks of entertainers because she didn't need to rely on the bonus track to sell her work. It also pointed out that her confidence in self-expression showed that she had matured as a performer.

After *My Everything* was released, a fourth single, "Love Me Harder," came out on September 30. This song featured Canadian artist The Weeknd and peaked at No. 7 on the *Billboard* Hot 100 in the United States, becoming Grande's fourth top-ten single of the year. In this song, the two singers trade verses about keeping her happy.

THE HONEYMOON TOUR

Grande's invitations to perform at industry events continued. On November 23, Grande performed at the

STAND UP TO CANCER

Stand Up to Cancer (SU2C) was founded in 2008 to bring the financial power and influence of the entertainment industry into the fight against cancer. Funds raised help pay for research into early discovery and treatments. An annual TV special brings together entertainers for this cause, and on September 5, 2014, this event included Grande. Grande sang "My Everything" in honor of her grandfather, who had died in July of cancer. She tweeted to her fans about how difficult the performance was, writing, "Sobbed my eyes out as soon as I got back."[6]

AMAs, singing acoustic versions of "Problems" and "Break Free" accompanied by only piano and saxophone. She then broke into "Love Me Harder," singing a duet with The Weeknd. Later, she joined Minaj and Jessie J to perform "Bang Bang."

A week after the release of *My Everything*, Grande announced her Honeymoon Tour, her first major concert tour. It would start on February 25, 2015, in Kansas City, Missouri, and travel through the United States, Canada, Europe, and South America. It would end in São Paulo, Brazil, on October 25. Timothy Finn of the *Kansas City Star* gave the opening show a glowing review, saying,

> *The show at the sold-out Independence Events Center was an extravagant mix of music, dance, lasers, videos, pyrotechnics and costume changes, akin to the kinds of audio-visual spectacles delivered by fellow pop-divas like Katy Perry and Britney Spears.*[7]

Finn went on to say that the only drop in energy came with a video visit by Imogen Heap, who explained the MiMU gloves she had designed for Grande. In the video, Heap explained that the gloves are designed to electronically alter Grande's voice and create a variety of effects, which Grande demonstrated while singing "Why Try."

During the worldwide Honeymoon Tour, Grande performed her song "Best Mistake" while standing on a cloud-shaped platform suspended from the ceiling.

Not all reviewers were as positive as Finn. Piet Levy of the *Milwaukee Journal* stated that Grande just wasn't ready for major stadium shows and that most of the time the show felt more like a dress rehearsal than a performance. He singled out "Why Try" and the use of the MiMU gloves, wondering why anyone felt the need to electronically alter Grande's voice. He praised her natural singing ability, calling the vocals during "My Everything" and "Just a Little Bit of Your Heart" sensational.

BACKYARD SESSIONS

Miley Cyrus created *The Backyard Sessions* as a YouTube series in which she sang covers and original music in a casual backyard setting. Grande joined her in May 2015 to sing a cover of "Don't Dream It's Over," a song originally performed by Crowded House. The videos included a link for fans to donate to the Happy Hippy Foundation, an organization founded by Cyrus to help homeless LGBTQ+ youth. Grande and Cyrus performed in footed pajamas while sitting on an inflatable couch with the band behind them. The song gave the two a chance to show off their lower vocal registers.

In April, she and boyfriend rapper Big Sean ended their relationship. They had been dating for about nine months. With both of them on tour, they simply couldn't make time to be together.

In June 2015, news outlets in the music industry reported that Grande had signed a contract with Universal Music Publishing Group (UMPG). This larger company owns Republic, which records and releases her music. UMPG represents artists and the licenses for their music when used in film and TV worldwide.

Jody Gerson is the chair and CEO at UMPG. She said, "We're so pleased to be working with her, alongside her management and our partners at Republic, to represent her songs and help maximize opportunities around the world."[8] While Republic represents Grande's work in the United States, UMPG represents it in the larger global market, which gives fans around the world better access to her work.

CHAPTER FIVE

A LITTLE MOONLIGHT

In May 2015, Grande was tweeting about moonlight and the moon. She even shared a photo of her latest tattoo, a small crescent moon. These posts were hinting about the name of her upcoming album. On May 29, she revealed that her third album would be titled *Moonlight*.

Grande's first single from the album, "Focus," was released on October 30, 2015. The song opens with the line "I know what I came to do, and that ain't gonna change."[1] Grande said this line is a nod to her mission in life, which is to make people feel happy, empowered, and not alone. Grande explained that when the chorus says, "Focus on me," she doesn't

Grande performed at Madison Square Garden in New York City on March 20, 2015. >>

mean focus on how she looks or that she wants to be the center of attention. She wants to emphasize that we need to focus on one another as people. The song reached No. 7 on the *Billboard* Hot 100 chart in the United States but was later cut from the album's track list because it didn't fit the feel of the album as a whole.

"OVER AND OVER AGAIN"

While she was working on *Moonlight*, Grande took the opportunity to sing a duet with Nathan Sykes on a remix of "Over and Over Again." The song was for his solo debut, *Unfinished Business*, which was released on November 11, 2016. Sykes said he heard the song playing in the UK and realized that Grande would sound great singing it. The other songs on the album are about heartbreak, but "Over and Over Again" is a love ballad.

DANGEROUS WOMAN

On March 11, 2016, Grande released a new single, "Dangerous Woman." She also announced that she was changing the title of the upcoming album to *Dangerous Woman* too. Fans asked her why, and Grande explained that she really loved the name *Moonlight*, and that its romance tied together her old music and her new music.

Despite this, she wanted to go with the stronger title of *Dangerous Woman* for the album. In addition to wanting to empower her fans, the sound of this new song

Grande's album *Dangerous Woman* had 15 songs, including "Moonlight," "Be Alright," and "Side To Side," a track featuring Nicki Minaj.

embodied her own growth. Unlike the pop sound of her earliest songs, "Dangerous Woman" features a guitar solo, synthesizer, and organ, creating depth and a sound similar to blues. "Dangerous Woman" climbed to No. 8 on the *Billboard* Hot 100 chart in the United States.

In addition to recording music, Grande had numerous opportunities to perform. On March 12, she hosted *Saturday Night Live* (*SNL*) and also performed as the musical guest. She sang "Dangerous Woman" and "Be Alright," a new promotional track. This song was released on March 18 but reached only 43 on the *Billboard* Hot 100 chart. In addition to her performances, she and the women of *SNL* were showcased in a humorous video called "This Is Not a Feminist Song." The skit stressed that it is so difficult to speak for all women that maybe they shouldn't even try or they'll risk being criticized.

The album *Dangerous Woman* was released on May 20. Writing in the *Guardian*, Michael Cragg described its sound, stating, "*Dangerous Woman* is a refinement of her sound, shifting from the low-slung groove of the title track and Moonlight's jazzy refrain, to the throbbing electro of new single Into You and the pulsating, future-assisted Everyday."[2]

Rolling Stone described Grande's style as all over the place but still complimented her voice. "[H]er phrasing remains unique and powerful and pyrotechnic, going at unexpected angles. . . . Grande may not have settled on a sound, but she's still an outsized, dangerous talent."[3] *Dangerous Woman* climbed to No. 2 on the *Billboard* 200 in the United States.

The TV show *Hairspray Live!* was an adaptation of the musical play that ran on Broadway.

HAIRSPRAY LIVE!

With the album successfully launched, Grande turned to acting. In December 2016, she played Penny Pingleton in a live televised version of the musical *Hairspray* that aired on NBC. The musical, which is set in the 1960s, is about Tracy, who wins a place on her favorite televised dance show. She sees it's unfair that Black kids can dance on the show only once a month and is determined to change this. *Variety* pointed out that it took a while to build up to the song and dance numbers, but then the energy kicked in.

Grande was praised for her performance as Penny. She starts off playing the part of a comedic sidekick before morphing into a showstopping diva. Grande had been offered four solos that would have been added to the show for her to perform, but she declined them, stating that she wanted to be faithful to the original. The production, although set in the 1960s, was praised for being relevant both for its themes of acceptance and positivity and also for not feeling dated, perhaps because of the inclusion of modern stars such as Grande.

THE TOUR

Grande's Dangerous Woman Tour launched on February 2, 2017, with a concert in Phoenix, Arizona.

EMPOWERING WOMEN

Grande is serious about empowering women. After multiple interviewers asked about her ex, Big Sean, she posted an essay on Twitter. Grande said she doesn't want to be identified as his ex or as anyone's girlfriend. "The double standard and misogyny are still ever present," she wrote, saying she wanted to be judged not for her romantic partner but for herself.[5] Grande feels that women need to be valued for who they are and not for whom they might be in a relationship with.

Writing for *Billboard*, Kristin Corpus reviewed the February 23 show in New York City. She praised Grande's staging and choreography as well as the projection of images and videos onto scrim. These projections, as described by Corpus, included a string of adjectives such as "sensual" and "loud" followed by "NOT ASKING FOR IT."[4] Corpus felt the meaning was clear—Grande was sending an anti-sexism message.

Longtime friend and collaborator Mac Miller joined Grande onstage during shows in Inglewood, California, and Paris, France, to perform their song "The Way." In the years since they had recorded the song, the two had remained close. They had started dating in September 2016.

On May 22, Grande played at the Manchester Arena in the United Kingdom. As the concert ended, a suicide bomber set off an explosion in the arena's foyer. The blast

In the wake of the bombing at Grande's show in Manchester, people lit candles and left flowers and balloons at the city's Saint Ann's Square in memory of those who lost their lives.

killed 22 people, including children.[6] Instead of playing the next two concerts scheduled for London, England, and additional concerts in Europe, Grande suspended the tour and returned to her hometown of Boca Raton. She refunded the money of fans who had already purchased tickets and posted messages of support and shock, expressing her sorrow over what had happened.

Grande wanted to do something to help the people affected by the bombing. "One Last Time" had been released in 2015, but Grande rereleased it for charity after the attack. It was the last song she had played during her Manchester concert. The proceeds from the sale of the

Grande performed with Miley Cyrus at the One Love Manchester fundraising concert on June 4, 2017.

song went into the We Love Manchester Emergency Fund. The fund itself was coordinated by the British Red Cross.

On June 4, Grande hosted an online concert, One Love Manchester, to benefit the people of Manchester. The event had a viewership of 10.9 million people, who tuned in to see performances by Miley Cyrus, Katy Perry, Justin Bieber, Coldplay, Imogen Heap, and many more. The event raised $3.5 million, which would be added to the $13 million in the We Love Manchester Emergency Fund to benefit the victims of the attack.[7]

Grande later explained in interviews that she never considered completely canceling the tour, although she did understand why some people would have made that decision. For her and for those working on her show, the tour's message of empowerment was simply too important, and people needed to hear it. After a two-week break, the tour resumed in June in Paris, France.

After Grande had rereleased the song, it became a rallying cry for her fans. During the Paris concert, Grande became emotional during the song and turned the chorus over to her fans to sing. She closed out this concert with "Somewhere over the Rainbow," one of the songs she performed for One Love Manchester.

The singer later admitted that she continued to suffer from post-traumatic stress disorder (PTSD) related to the bombing. When she spoke about her PTSD to *British Vogue*, she also said she felt guilty talking about the struggles she had following the bombing. "I know those families and my fans, and everyone there experienced a tremendous amount of it as well," Grande said.[8]

CHRISTMAS & CHILL

In December 2015, Grande released her second Christmas EP. *Christmas & Chill* contained six original songs, and Grande tweeted that it took her and her team less than a week to create the album. *Rolling Stone* described *Christmas & Chill* as R&B leaning except for the final track, titled "Winter Things." *Rolling Stone* called the track folkie and pointed out that it is acoustic. This song has no electronic instruments but does include a ukelele. In this song, the Boca Raton native sings about how she isn't going to let hot weather melt away her Christmas spirit.

CHAPTER SIX

SWEETENER

On February 14, 2018, there was a shooting at Marjory Stoneman Douglas High School in Parkland, Florida. A gunman killed 17 people and injured 17 others.[1] Reacting to this tragedy, students from the school took part in a March 24 protest in Washington, DC, called March for Our Lives.

The protesters wanted to strengthen gun control laws. Several singers contributed performances to the protest, including Grande. She prefaced "Be Alright" with a statement thanking everyone who was working for change and a safe future.

In addition to helping causes important to her, Grande was working on a new album. She was collaborating with singer and songwriter Pharrell Williams, who was producing the album. Grande complimented Williams on how easy he was to

Grande performed at the March for Our Lives event in Washington, DC, which drew an estimated 200,000 people. >>

WE CALL BS.

Pharrell Williams produced about half the songs that appeared on Grande's album *Sweetener* in 2018.

work with. She said he didn't come into the project with an ego but instead spent time learning more about her as a person. "He was more worried about getting to know me and making sure I was comfortable," she said.[2]

Grande spoke to reporters about a time when she was explaining her emotions to Williams and he started working on the title track. Williams, who was also present at the interview, explained that his job is a lot like being a stenographer who has to figure out the singer's emotion and match that with the work. He said that is why it is so important for Grande to be relaxed. "If she's not comfortable, she's never going to give me the pure her," Williams said.[3]

SINGLES

Grande released her single "No Tears Left to Cry" on April 20. It was her first release since the Manchester concert bombing the previous May. In the studio, she told her team that she wanted a song like Gloria Gaynor's "I Will Survive" that starts out as a slow ballad and then becomes something else. She told them she wanted the song to be positive because she simply didn't have any tears left.

MTV VIDEO MUSIC AWARDS

Grande was nominated for five MTV VMAs in 2018. In addition to her nomination for Best Artist of the Year, she was nominated for four awards for "No Tears Left to Cry." These awards were Best Pop Video, Best Video of the Year, Best Visual Effects, and Best Cinematography, which is the art of lighting, composing, and framing camera shots. She won Best Pop Video and performed "God Is a Woman." The awards were held on August 20, the same night as Grande's New York City concert, which she played after the VMAs.

The song doesn't specifically reference Manchester, but in the last seconds of the video, a worker bee, a symbol of the city, flies toward the camera. The song reached No. 3 on the *Billboard* Hot 100 chart in the United States. "No Tears Left to Cry" went on to win Best Pop Video at the MTV Video Music Awards (VMAs) in 2018 and the *NME* Best Song of 2018. *NME* is a British pop culture magazine. About "No Tears Left to Cry," *NME* said, "This defiant return was the year's best pop song,

Grande attended the VMAs with Mac Miller on August 28, 2016.

proof of music's oft-touted healing properties and of the empowerment of dusting yourself off and starting again."[4]

In May 2018, Grande and Mac Miller broke up. The two remained friends after the relationship ended. Grande posted about Miller on social media, stating, "I respect and adore him endlessly and am grateful to have him in my life in any form, at all times regardless of how our relationship changes or what the universe holds for each of us!"[5]

Grande continued to work with other artists. On June 13, Australia's Troye Sivan released "Dance to This," a song featuring Grande. Although he and Grande had known each other for about two years, he admitted that he had been nervous to ask her to sing with him. He explained that when he collaborates, he worries the other person might not like his song. The duet is about a couple who would rather stay home than go out and dance.

The next day, Nicki Minaj dropped "Bed," a single that featured Grande. The track would be part of Minaj's fourth album, *Queen*. In this song, Grande croons the R&B chorus and Minaj raps the verses. Minaj had already written the chorus when Grande visited her in the studio, offering to sing on a song for the new album. It wasn't until Grande left that Minaj thought of the chorus and sent it to her. Grande recorded it with harmonies and runs and sent it back to Minaj.

Grande's single "God Is a Woman" was released on July 18 and became her tenth top-ten single, peaking at No. 8 on the *Billboard* Hot 100 in the United States. The song is about female sexuality, empowerment, and spirituality. Songwriter Savan Kotecha had the original idea for the song and tried to think of who

LAWSUIT

While many people who objected to the song "God Is a Woman" were offended by the idea that God is female, Vladimir Kush and his company Kush Fine Art Las Vegas filed a lawsuit over something else entirely. The lawsuit stated that in the video for the song, the image of Grande in a candle flame was copied from a painting he did in 1999 or 2000. Kush wanted not only a monetary settlement but also for Grande to remove the video that was posted online. Grande settled the case out of court, and the video remains available.

might be willing to make such a radical statement. He bounced the idea off Grande, thinking she would partner with a rapper who would rap the chorus. But Grande decided to do the chorus, "You'll believe God is a woman," herself. Then she went home and recorded a rough demo of the song.

THE ALBUM AND THE TOUR

Grande's new album, *Sweetener,* was released on August 17, 2018. By September 1 it had reached No. 1 on the *Billboard* 200 chart of top-selling albums. Nine songs from the album charted on the *Billboard* Hot 100. She also had a collaboration, Minaj's "Bed," on the Hot 100, so Grande became the fourth female artist to reach the mark of ten songs on the chart at the same time, following Taylor Swift, Beyoncé, and Cardi B.

Shortly before *Sweetener* was released, Grande changed the name of the last track from "Pete" to "Pete Davidson." The pair dated and had been engaged for about four months. But in October 2018, they separated.

Reaching No. 1 with *Sweetener* gave her a third No. 1 album, following *Yours Truly* and *My Everything*. *Dangerous Woman* had peaked at No. 2. With *Sweetener,* Grande also had the second-best week of sales for a

Grande and Pete Davidson attended the VMAs in August 2018. The couple had moved into an apartment together in New York City before deciding to break up.

female artist in 2018, topped only by Cardi B and her album *Invasion of Privacy*.

Most of the reviews Grande received for *Sweetener* were positive. *Entertainment Weekly* described it as "a fascinating and sneakily complex pop album that adds new creative wrinkles to Grande's already estimable repertoire."[6] The *AV Club* website wrote, "Confident and empowered, *Sweetener* illustrates once again that Grande

During the Sweetener Sessions performances, Grande frequently sat on a stool for a more casual, relaxed show.

is an unparalleled pop chameleon."[7] None of the reviews were completely negative, but some were lukewarm. The *Guardian*'s review said, "It sounds like the work of an artist torn between doing exactly what she pleases and, perhaps understandably under the circumstances, giving her audience what they want."[8]

ARIANA GRANDE AT THE BBC

On November 1, 2018, the British Broadcasting Corporation (BBC) aired a one-hour special that marked the first time Grande had appeared on the network since One Love Manchester. In this televised event, Grande sang accompanied by a female orchestra and then sat down to an interview with the BBC's Davina McCall. The pair discussed music, inspiration, and the Manchester tragedy. McCall asked Grande to name her favorite song. Grande chose "Hide and Seek" by Imogen Heap.

Only three days after the release of *Sweetener*, Grande launched a series of shows called the Sweetener Sessions, holding four concerts in New York City, Los Angeles, London, and Chicago, Illinois. The concerts took place between August 20 and September 4. New York City's concert was in Irving Plaza, a venue with only 1,000 seats.

At the concert, Grande announced to her fans that there really wasn't a plan and that they would get to select the order of the songs. Based on their reactions, "Breathin" took the lead as the opening number. Grande wrapped up the event with "No Tears Left to Cry."

CHAPTER SEVEN

HER OWN RULES

When Grande spoke to *Billboard* in 2018, she told her interviewer that she wanted to be able to release music in the same way rappers did. She disliked the regimented way that female pop artists had to release their work. First, they had to tease fans, letting them know that new music would soon be released, and then release a single. Once the song was released, they had to allow time for radio play to generate buzz before releasing a video, with everything meticulously scheduled.

What Grande wanted to do was create music as quickly as possible and release it just as quickly. She wanted to benefit from streaming and the

Grande has become known for standing up for herself >> and others. She has waved a pride flag onstage to show her support of the LGBTQ+ community.

DANGEROUS WOMAN DIARIES

On November 29, 2018, Grande released a four-part documentary series called *Ariana Grande: Dangerous Woman Diaries* on YouTube. Each episode was approximately 30 minutes long. The series explored how the *Sweetener* album was a reaction to the Dangerous Woman Tour, Grande's creative process, how she and her crew managed being on the road, and her decision to put on the One Love Manchester concert. New episodes dropped on Thursdays to keep her fans coming back regularly to learn more about her work and her creative life.

opportunity it offers for rapid releases, inundating fans with as much music as possible. Rappers often release a large number of songs all at once through streaming services because many radio stations refuse to play their work. They have to use streaming and social media to reach potential fans.

Grande isn't in this situation, but she wanted the freedom to use streaming and social media to her benefit. "To drop a record on a Saturday night because you feel like it. . . . If I want to tour two albums at once, I'm going to tour two albums at once. If I want to drop a third album while I'm on tour [in 2019], I'll do that too!"[1] And that's just what she did.

THE ALBUM

Grande released "Thank U, Next," the first single from her upcoming album of the same name, on November 3, 2018.

This song was about self-empowerment and Grande's starting a new chapter in her life. In it, she thanked her various ex-boyfriends, including rapper Big Sean, dancer Ricky Alvarez, rapper Mac Miller, and comedian Pete Davidson. When the song debuted, 829,000 fans streamed the video, which she released at the same time, setting a new YouTube premiere record.[2]

In one scene of the music video, Grande is driving a convertible with a license plate that reads "7 Rings." This led to rumors. Fans speculated about what this might have meant until Grande revealed that she was teasing another song on the album. "Thank U, Next" became Grande's first song to reach No. 1 on the *Billboard* Hot 100 chart in the United States. Before "Thank U, Next," her highest debuting song was "Problem," her collaboration with Iggy Azalea, which hit the charts at No. 3.

On January 18, 2019, "7 Rings" became the next song from the album to debut. Grande explained that after a breakup, she took six friends to Tiffany's, a famous high-end jewelry store in New York, where she bought them all matching rings. One of these friends suggested that Grande turn the event into a song.

The day it debuted, "7 Rings" accrued nearly 15 million global plays on Spotify, beating the previous record

NO. 1 ON THE *BILLBOARD* HOT 100

Ariana Grande has had nine songs that have climbed to the No. 1 spot on the *Billboard* Hot 100 chart.

Song	Release Date	Weeks at No. 1
"Die For You"	Dec. 17, 2016	1
"Thank U, Next"	Nov. 17, 2018	7
"7 Rings"	Feb. 2, 2019	8
"Save Your Tears"	Apr. 4, 2020	2
"Stuck With U"	May 23, 2020	1
"Rain on Me"	June 6, 2020	1
"Positions"	Nov. 7, 2020	1
"Yes, And?"	Jan. 27, 2024	1
"We Can't Be Friends (Wait for Your Love)"	Mar. 23, 2024	1

for streams on a single day. This record had been set by Mariah Carey for "All I Want for Christmas Is You," which nearly 11 million fans streamed on Spotify on December 24, 2018.[3] In her song, Grande sings about retail therapy and seeing something, liking it, and buying it, including her hair. Fans embraced the sentiment, and this song also went to No. 1 on the *Billboard* Hot 100 chart in the United States.

"Break Up with Your Girlfriend, I'm Bored" was the third song from *Thank U, Next* that was released as a single. It is about a woman who is infatuated with a man she's never met. The song debuted at No. 2 on the *Billboard* Hot 100 chart in the United States and came out on February 23, 2019, the same day as the album.

Thank U, Next was released less than five months after *Sweetener.* Grande said that in many ways it was an album she had to make. It was a chance to reflect on the September 2018 death of her ex and friend Mac Miller and her breakup with Pete Davidson.

During this time, she was also still having panic attacks and dealing with depression as a result of the Manchester bombing. She needed to be with friends and work through her feelings with music. The album's songs were written and recorded in only two weeks by Grande and her team, including producer Tommy Brown, songwriter Justin Tranter, and singer-songwriter Njomza.

AWARDS

In their first week, the songs on *Thank U, Next* had 59 million streams, which set the record for the most album streams in a single week by a female artist.[4] *Thank U, Next* was nominated for a People's Choice Award, an AMA, and two Grammys. With this album, Grande also became the first artist since the Beatles to hold the top three slots of the *Billboard* Hot 100 chart.

In February 2019, one of the producers of the Grammy Awards said in an interview that Grande had decided not to perform at the awards that year because, by the time they had agreed on what she would do, she felt it was too late to put together a performance. When she saw this, Grande immediately told her fans that this had not been the problem at all. Instead, she had suggested three different songs she could perform, and the producers told her to do a medley, which is a mix of several songs in one.

COLLABORATION

Many people collaborate, or work together, to create an album like *Thank U, Next*. After the album was released, songwriter Justin Tranter, who worked with Grande on the album, spoke with National Public Radio (NPR) Music. He discussed what Grande's level of engagement meant to him. "It was so inspiring to me to see how in charge and how involved she is every step of the way, from the writing to the vision to the storytelling and to even engineering and comping her own vocals," he said.[6] Comping involves recording several takes of a song and combining the best parts.

"It's about collaboration. It's about feeling supported. It's about art and honesty, not politics," wrote Grande on Twitter.[5] Grande decided not to attend the award ceremony although she had been nominated in two categories. This was the year she won her first Grammy, Best Pop Vocal Album for *Sweetener*.

Grande appeared as if she were singing beneath a full moon on the opening night of the Sweetener World Tour at Times Union Center in Albany, New York, on March 18, 2019.

THE SWEETENER WORLD TOUR

Grande kicked off the Sweetener World Tour in New York on March 18, 2019, performing songs from both *Sweetener* and *Thank U, Next*. The song list included 31 of her hits, but there were songs that were notably absent, including "Ghostin" and "Imagine," two songs about Mac Miller. Grande said these songs were simply too painful to perform at that time. She paid homage to Miller by playing his music as fans entered the venue.

It was up to LeRoy Bennett, as the concert tour's creative director and production designer, to create the look that Grande wanted. She told him she liked the idea

Grande's merchandise tent at the Coachella music festival featured a tunnel made of seven rings.

of a sphere, which she associates with the universe and femininity. The first spherical area that fans noticed was the pit. It was a sunken area in front of the main stage that was surrounded by a horseshoe-shaped walkway. Fans in this pit got an up-close look at Grande during the concert.

Bennett included a spherical projection screen behind the stage as well as an orb that was lowered over the pit for "Goodnight n Go" and "Get Well Soon." Projectors made the orb look like the moon. Bennett told reporters that it took six to eight hours to set everything up before a concert and another four hours to take it all down again.

The 2019 *Billboard* Music Awards took place during the tour. Grande received nine nominations. She won both Top Female Artist and the *Billboard* Chart Achievement Award, which is one of the categories voted on by fans. Then she performed via prerecorded video because she was on tour.

The tour continued through December and included 97 concerts, along with performances at the music festivals Coachella and Lollapalooza. This was Grande's biggest tour ever. By the time the tour was over, she had earned $146.4 million and sold 1.3 million concert tickets.[7]

The day after the final concert, December 23, 2019, Grande released a new album. *K Bye for Now (SWT Live)* consisted of 32 tracks with guest appearances by Nicki Minaj and Big Sean. Recorded throughout the tour, this was Grande's first live album.

Grande was making a name for herself as a musician and earning money from album sales, individual streams, and concert tickets. Each year, the business magazine *Forbes* ranks the 100 highest-paid celebrities in the world. In 2019, Grande was on the *Forbes* list at number 17, having earned an estimated $72 million that year.[8]

COACHELLA

For two weekends in April 2019, Grande headlined Coachella, the annual music festival held at Empire Polo Club in Indio, California. At age 25, Grande was the youngest female singer to do so and only the fourth woman. Grande brought a variety of performers to the event, including Nicki Minaj and Justin Bieber, who joined her onstage. Members of NSYNC, with the exception of Justin Timberlake, came back together to perform with her as well. When NSYNC took the stage, Grande said, "Coachella, I've been waiting my whole life for this moment."[9]

CHAPTER EIGHT

POSITIONS

As Grande was wrapping up her Sweetener World Tour in late 2019, the first cases of what would later be identified as the COVID-19 illness were beginning to surface in Wuhan, China. This highly contagious illness was declared a pandemic in March 2020. Schools, day care centers, and businesses closed. Many people stayed home in an effort to slow the spread of the disease. Millions of people lost their jobs.

A number of celebrities stepped forward, making donations to further medical research into the pandemic and providing aid to those who needed help. Grande checked out the tweets of her fans and looked for people who were struggling. When she found someone who needed aid, including people who had lost jobs in retail, she sent them money via

Grande performed at the O2 Arena in London, England, in August 2019, toward the end of the Sweetener Tour. >>

Grande and Justin Bieber have been friends since at least 2010 and have collaborated on projects ever since.

the Venmo app. The amounts varied between $500 and $1,500 per person.[1]

In April 2020, politicians Stacey Abrams and Andrew Yang announced the formation of Project 100. With this initiative, they gathered donations to provide $1,000 digital payments to 100,000 families that relied on public assistance such as food stamps and had been severely impacted by the pandemic.[2] Grande, Rihanna, and other celebrities supported this effort.

Grande and Justin Bieber collaborated on "Stuck With U," a single about being stuck with a new boyfriend or girlfriend while self-isolating during the pandemic. Grande and Bieber put together a homemade music video that compiled photographs and videos of each of them in lockdown at home, as well as photographs and videos sent in by their fans.

The people in some of the clips were celebrity friends who had also sent in quarantine videos. These included actors Ashton Kutcher and Gwyneth Paltrow, Chance the Rapper, and singer Michael Bublé. Fans who watched the video closely also caught sight of Dalton Gomez, Grande's boyfriend at the time. She sheltered with him during the early part of the pandemic. Grande and Bieber donated the money from the sale of the single to the First Responders Children's Foundation, which gave grants and scholarships to the children of first responders working throughout the pandemic. The song was released on May 8.

MERRY CHRISTMAS!

Grande's generosity didn't end with COVID assistance. As Christmas neared in 2020, she and her team picked out a variety of gifts for hospitalized children. Many of the gifts went to babies, children, and teens in four Los Angeles hospitals. "Because we treat so many different ages and a spectrum of unique needs, she was very deliberate and intentional in making sure every child and family was taken care of," said staff at the UCLA Mattel Children's Hospital.[3] In addition to toys for young patients, pizzas were delivered for staff.

THE ALBUM

"Positions," Grande's first single from her upcoming album of the same name, was released on October 23, 2020.

The song features synthesized trap beats and Grande's R&B and pop vibe. The song reached No. 1 on the *Billboard* Hot 100 chart in the United States. Critics praised it as a bold introduction to her new music, calling it delightfully simple and catchy.

The album *Positions* was released on October 30 to many positive reviews. Mary Siroky of the website *Consequence of Sound* called it showy and wildly theatrical, full of romance and flirtation. Ross Horton of the music website the *Line of Best Fit* called it Grande's most mature work to date and praised its carefree, playful tone.

Shaad D'Souza of the website the *Fader* was significantly less generous, declaring that *Positions* was Grande's first real miss. D'Souza called the album vague and tiresome. In an interview with *People* magazine,

"POSITIONS" VIDEO

On the surface, "Positions" is a song about the various roles a woman plays in the home, but Grande's music video makes it clear that the song is about much more than that. In the video, Grande is the president of the United States and even wears a suit reminiscent of those worn by Jackie Kennedy, the wife of President John F. Kennedy. Even in the White House, Grande spends time creating in the kitchen, sending a message that a woman can be whatever she wants to be. Grande's mother, Joan Grande, is one of the people playing Grande's presidential advisers in the video.

Grande said she would have done a lot more with the album prior to its release if she had felt her fans were really into it, but instead she felt the fans were telling her, "This is not what we want."[4] Despite this and some negative reviews, the album debuted at No. 1 on the *Billboard* Top 200.

The album's second single, "34+35," was released on November 3, 2020, after the album. Grande was concerned that, because the lyrics are overtly sexual, releasing the song as the lead single could detract from the tone of the rest of the album. This was why she led with "Positions," which she saw as a better fit. She also found it humorous that "34+35" includes strings, which sound very proper and refined, when the actual lyrics are raunchy.

Grande later worked with Doja Cat and Megan Thee Stallion to create a remix of "34+35," which was released on January 15, 2021. Horton praised the song for its humor, double entendre, and puns. D'Souza, on the other hand, said that the song doesn't even try to be vaguely clever. The song was

> "This is the point, you put art there so that people can tear it apart and do whatever they want with it, or celebrate it or whatever."[5]
>
> —Ariana Grande on negative responses to *Positions*, November 6, 2024

popular with listeners, climbing to No. 3 on the UK Singles Chart and to No. 2 on the *Billboard* Hot 100 chart in the United States.

The third single from *Positions* was called "POV" and was released on March 23, 2021. This song is a quiet R&B ballad accompanied by cello and viola. It debuted at No. 40 on the *Billboard* Hot 100 before climbing to No. 27 in the United States. The song was praised by critics, with Siroky calling it one of the three essential pieces on the album, along with "My Hair" and "Six Thirty."

MUSIC AND MORE

In December 2020, Grande appeared in *Don't Look Up*, a dark comedy film about an asteroid heading toward Earth. In the movie, scientists detect the incoming asteroid but have a hard time persuading people to take action against it. It satirizes politics, the media, and the public's obsession with celebrities.

Grande plays pop star Riley Bina, who is in a relationship with a rapper played by Scott Mescudi, who is also known as Kid Cudi. The film stars Leonardo DiCaprio, Jennifer Lawrence, and Meryl Streep in the lead roles. In addition to appearing in the movie, Grande and Mescudi recorded the song "Just Look Up." The movie set

In *Don't Look Up*, Grande made up her own lyrics to the movie's theme song during the first take. The director loved it and kept it in the film.

viewership records when it was released on the streaming service Netflix.

In May 2021, Grande and Gomez married in a small ceremony with only about 20 guests. It took place in their home in Montecito, California. Grande kept her marriage out of the media, preferring to keep that part of her life private. Their separation and divorce were just as private. The couple agreed on a divorce settlement in October 2023, and the divorce was final in March 2024.

THE VOICE

In September 2021, Grande joined the twenty-first season of the singing competition show *The Voice* as a coach. In a preview video, Grande said that she was moved by the dedication the competitors showed to their craft. Despite her enthusiasm, Grande served in this role for only one season, declining to return. She revealed in an interview that coaching was a lot of work, and although she really enjoyed it, she tended to get too emotionally attached to everyone on her team. She recognized this as her own problem and decided not to return.

Grande continued to feature in the work of other artists. "Die for You" was the fifth single released from The Weeknd's 2016 album *Starboy*. It peaked at No. 43 on the *Billboard* Hot 100 during its initial release. In 2021, the song began gaining popularity on the video-sharing service TikTok. On February 24, 2023, The Weeknd released a new remix featuring Grande. This was the fourth time they had collaborated, and Grande's harmonies and vocal runs helped push the remix to No. 1 on the *Billboard* Hot 100 chart, making it the seventh No. 1 song for each of them.

To celebrate the tenth anniversary of *Yours Truly*, Grande released a deluxe edition on August 25, 2023. In addition to the studio tracks, it includes Live from London tracks, versions of several songs that had been recorded in 2018 when she performed in London at the BBC in front of a small studio audience. There was also a new version of

Grande and The Weeknd sang "Save Your Tears" at the 2021 iHeartRadio Music Awards in Los Angeles, California.

"The Way," featuring the late Mac Miller. It alternated between English and Spanish lyrics.

Grande also released videos for "Honeymoon Avenue" and "Daydreamin'." Both videos were recorded when she was performing Live from London. Grande held question-and-answer sessions with fans and released a vinyl picture disc of the album. This was a vinyl record with a picture of Grande on it.

CHAPTER NINE

THE MET AND MORE

On January 12, 2024, even before Grande had announced that she was working on another album, the single "Yes, And?" was released. It is a song about being resilient and having the self-confidence to heal. She sings about following her own path and ignoring body shaming and gossip. Grande has always rejected people's comments about her body.

She had recently endured gossip about her relationship with her new boyfriend, Ethan Slater, so soon after separating from Gomez. Grande wrote "Yes, And?" with Max Martin and Ilya Salmanzadeh, although Salmanzadeh told *Billboard* that when they started, Grande already knew which emotions she

Grande met actor and singer Ethan Slater on the set of *Wicked*, and the two began dating in July 2023. >>

wanted the song to evoke. The song debuted atop the *Billboard* Hot 100.

"We Can't Be Friends (Wait for Your Love)," written by Grande, was the second single from her upcoming album *Eternal Sunshine*. It debuted on March 8, 2024. The music video references the movie *Eternal Sunshine of the Spotless Mind*, which inspired the album's title.

"YES, AND?"

The title of Grande's song "Yes, And?" comes from a common phrase in improvisational theater, where actors work together to make up a scene as they go along. One person starts by saying or doing something. Another actor will help create the scene by building on what the first person has done. Approaching the scene with a collaborative mindset of saying, "Yes, and?" to the other performers helps the scene flow smoothly. Grande explained to Amazon Music that the title is about staying positive and always moving forward.

In the video, Grande plays a character named Peaches, who goes to a clinic to have all memories of her boyfriend removed from her mind so she can move on. This is similar to what happens in the film. The song debuted at the top of the *Billboard* Hot 100 chart in the United States.

Eternal Sunshine was released on the same day as "We Can't Be Friends (Wait for Your Love)." It had been four years since the release of her previous album, *Positions*. *Eternal Sunshine* explores romance and partnership. The album debuted at No. 1 on the *Billboard* 200 chart in the United States, making it Grande's sixth album to achieve this. By September, the RIAA had certified the album as Platinum. Because *Eternal Sunshine* produced multiple No. 1 hits, Grande became the first woman to accomplish this on two albums. *Positions* also had multiple No. 1 hits.

On March 11, Grande released what she called the "Slightly Deluxe" version of *Eternal Sunshine.* It had four different versions of songs from the original album. The bonus tracks were a version of "Yes, And?" sung as a duet with Mariah Carey; "Supernatural," on which Grande collaborates with Troye Sivan; an acoustic version of "Imperfect For You;" and an a cappella version of "True Story."

When *Eternal Sunshine* was released, Grande's music wasn't supposed to be on TikTok due to a licensing dispute between TikTok and Universal Music Group. This meant songs were not officially uploaded by the Universal Music Group or a representative. When songs are officially uploaded, TikTok pays the artist each time their song is used in a video.

Although *Eternal Sunshine* wasn't officially on TikTok, fans could still share individual songs by playing

Grande met Troye Sivan at the 2016 *Billboard* Music Awards, and they have been friends and collaborators ever since.

them in the background. "The Boy Is Mine" is the eighth track on *Eternal Sunshine* and became part of a TikTok dance challenge that helped make the song more popular. On June 7, about three months after the album's release, Grande released "The Boy Is Mine" as a single and a music video.

The song is about two women competing for the affections of one man. In the video, the city is plagued by rats, so the mayor decides to release cats to solve the problem. Grande's nerdy character develops a love potion. She dresses as the comic book character Catwoman and goes after the mayor. "The Boy Is Mine" peaked at No. 16 on the *Billboard* Hot 100 in the United States.

THE LAST WORD

Grande's grandmother, Marjorie, has the last word in the song "Ordinary Things." ***Eternal Sunshine*** **opens with the question "How do I know if I'm in the right relationship?" The answer comes at the end of the last song on the album. Marjorie says, "Never go to bed without kissing goodnight. That's the worst thing to do. Don't ever, ever, ever do that. And if you can't, and if you don't feel comfortable doing it, you're in the wrong place. Get out."[1]**

THE MET GALA

In May 2024, Grande had an opportunity to perform at the Met Gala. As someone transfixed by fashion, this event was an excellent fit for Grande. The Met Gala is held every year on the first Monday in May. The event brings out celebrities and designers to raise funds to benefit New York City's Metropolitan Museum of Art Costume Institute. In 2024, the event celebrated the institute's latest exhibit, "Sleeping Beauties: Reawakening Fashion."

Photographers snap pictures of the stars as they walk the red carpet, turning the event into its own high fashion show. Grande was in her element. On May 6, she arrived at the event in a flowing off-white gown designed by Loewe and later changed into a more elaborate gown designed by John Galliano for her surprise performance. The top layer of the Galliano gown was white crinoline with a slim-fitting draped green dress sprayed with gold dust beneath.

Grande began her performance surrounded by 30 dancers, each with handheld mirrors. Her opening song was "Once Upon a Dream" from Disney's 1939 film *Sleeping Beauty*. After the first song, Grande removed the top gown to reveal the green dress underneath. She sang a medley of her hits, including "Into You" and "7 Rings."

For the final number, Grande was joined onstage by Cynthia Erivo, her costar in the upcoming movie *Wicked*. Together they sang "When You Believe," a song about faith and belief leading to miracles, famously sung by

Grande performed a seven-song medley at the 2024 Met Gala.

Mariah Carey and Whitney Houston for the 1998 movie *The Prince of Egypt*. Grande later commented on TikTok, "Working on this performance was an experience I will cherish forever." In a social media caption, she wrote, "Thank you to the divine and magical @cynthiaerivo for joining me in the end and for lighting up the museum brighter than any star in the sky ever could."[2]

MY EVERYTHING

On August 22, Grande celebrated the tenth anniversary of her album *My Everything* by releasing new editions, including one on pink vinyl and a new digital deluxe version of the album. The digital album was the first time fans could stream "Too Close" and "Cadillac Song." Grande announced the anniversary of the album on Instagram along with a special message for her fans.

"I love you all so much and am deeply grateful always. Hope you enjoy these little anniversary celebration surprises."[3]

On October 1, 2024, Grande released another version of *Eternal Sunshine*. The new deluxe album was called *Eternal Sunshine (Slightly Deluxe and Also Live)*. This album added live versions of "Intro (End of the World)," "Don't Wanna Break Up Again," "Eternal Sunshine," "Supernatural," "Imperfect for You," "Yes, And?," and "We Can't Be Friends (Wait for Your Love)." Videos of the live performances were released over the course of a week on her YouTube channel.

HER MET GALA LOOK

Grande's red-carpet dress at the 2024 Met Gala included a mother-of-pearl bodice, which was meaningful to her since pearl is her birthstone. "The inspiration for my look was the magic of nature and the many ways that it can surprise us," says Grande. "Something so beautiful can be born when you least expect it or in the most unexpected places, like a pearl." She explained that it was also meaningful because pearls reflect light. Grande sees pearls as "picking up on the pretty colors that they see and shining them right back at you."[4] She loved this imagery.

CHAPTER TEN

THE BIG SCREEN

On November 6, 2024, Grande announced in an interview that she planned to scale back her music output. She emphasized that she wasn't going to quit making music, but she was not going to release it at the rate she had been over the past ten years. Working on *Wicked* had helped Grande reignite her love of musicals, and she decided to look for more roles that could showcase both her acting and her singing skills.

Grande was about ten years old when her mother took her to see *Wicked* with the original cast on Broadway. Grande told an NBC interviewer that her mother had won backstage passes for the

Grande had loved the story of *The Wizard of Oz* since she was a child, so she really wanted to win the role of Galinda, who later becomes Glinda the Good, in *Wicked*. >>

ARIANA GRANDE is GLINDA
WICKED
NOVEMBER 22

ARIANA GRANDE-BUTERA

As Grande started her singing career, she used the name Ariana Grande. When she appeared in the film version of *Wicked*, she asked to be credited by her full name, Ariana Grande-Butera. She said the role helped her recall who she was when she first saw *Wicked*. Grande explained, "I do feel like this role and this project helped me sort of come home to little Ari. Maybe little pieces of her got lost along the way in this crazy industry, and I'm so grateful for the ways in which this experience led me back."[1]

show through a charity auction. She and her mother were able to meet the stars of the original Broadway show, including Kristin Chenoweth, who played Galinda.

In the story, Galinda later becomes Glinda the Good. During the meeting, Grande sang part of the song "Popular" from *Wicked*, and Chenoweth gave her both a wand and some shower gel she said was magical. Grande admitted that she hadn't wanted to use the gel up, so she had dipped her pinky into it every day. She said in the interview that maybe that gel really was magical, because it led her to the role in the film adaptation of the musical.

GETTING THE PART

Jon M. Chu is an American producer, director, and writer known for the hit 2018 film *Crazy Rich Asians*. In 2021, Universal Pictures brought on Chu to do a two-movie adaptation of *Wicked*. In 2022, he explained on Twitter why it would be two movies instead of one. "Here's what happened: as we prepared this production over the last year, it became increasingly clear that it would be impossible to wrestle the story of 'Wicked' into a single film without doing some real damage to it," wrote Chu.[2]

When Grande auditioned for Chu, there was a mix-up. In interviews, Grande had said she was interested in playing Galinda. But when the time came to audition for *Wicked*, the casting directors decided she should audition for Elphaba, so that was the part she prepared for.

Chu let her sing Elphaba's songs but found out she wanted to be Galinda. It was a relief for both of them because he hadn't wanted her to play Elphaba. Grande thinks the source of the confusion may have been because she had performed "The Wizard and I," one of Elphaba's songs, in 2018 for a fifteenth anniversary celebration of the Broadway show.

> **"This music has always brought such comfort and now being able to spend time with it and be trusted with it is the privilege of a lifetime."**[3]
>
> **—Ariana Grande on performing in *Wicked*, November 20, 2024**

Grande was cast to play Galinda Upland of the Upper Uplands, who is overly confident and irrepressible and the most popular girl at Shiz University. Galinda comes

Galinda gifts Elphaba a black hat, which becomes a symbol of their bond and Elphaba's individuality.

from a life of privilege, but more than anything, she wants magical power, something that money and privilege cannot buy. Elphaba, who is the only person in Oz with green skin and has uncontrollable powers, is assigned as her roommate.

FILMING

Wicked was filmed at Sky Studios Elstree outside of London. Grande and Erivo prepared for the film by getting to know each other, spending five hours hanging out at Erivo's apartment. "We had a real conversation right off the bat about creating a safe space for each other and being honest with each other," Grande said.[4]

The story deals with loss as the characters struggle to be themselves despite societal expectations. It also addresses having to leave people behind. As Galinda, Grande had to portray emotions of loss. "Losing someone you love is something we've all unfortunately had to experience—and sometimes we have the privilege to say goodbye, and sometimes we don't," Grande said.[5]

Chu decided the songs should be sung live instead of being dubbed later. "Live singing affected the entire mood of the set," cinematographer Alice Brooks told *NBC Insider*. Hearing the music performed live energized everyone working on the film. It even brought people to tears during highly emotional songs such as "Defying Gravity." "Everyone could feel that energy, and they all knew we were making something really special," Brooks said.[6]

Grande and Erivo did their own stunts. On *The Tonight Show*, Grande discussed her stunt during the song "Popular" when she is swinging around on a chandelier. "One of our stunt coordinators was

SATURDAY NIGHT LIVE

On October 12, 2024, Grande hosted *Saturday Night Live* (*SNL*) to promote *Wicked*. The musical guest for the night was Stevie Nicks. NBC reported it was the most-watched *SNL* episode ever on Peacock across its first two days of viewing. In "Bridesmaid Speech," Grande sings an off-key song about a bachelorette trip. In "Celine Dion Sports Promo," she demonstrates her talent for mimicking the vocal style and movements of other singers. These songs were written for the episode.

standing in the room just to make sure that I didn't break all of my limbs," Grande said before admitting that she accidentally kicked him.[7]

REVIEWS

Wicked was released on November 22, 2024. By May 19, 2025, it had grossed $755.8 million worldwide. This made it the top-earning film based on a Broadway musical, a record previously held by *Mama Mia!*, which grossed $611.5 million worldwide after its release in June 2008.[8]

The film as a whole received mixed reviews, earning four stars from Peter Bradshaw of the *Guardian*, who praised it as a "blast of entertainment power."[9] This contrasted sharply with the two stars the movie received from Robbie Collins of the *Telegraph*, who said there was no reason to divide the Broadway show into two films.

Grande and Erivo became good friends while filming *Wicked*. In 2025, the two actors continued to keep in touch, talking on the phone nearly every day.

While the film's reception was mixed, reviewers praised both Grande and Erivo. The *Hollywood Reporter* said the casting of Grande and Erivo was what made the movie a winner. *Digital Spy* complimented Grande's comic timing, which shines through especially well in "Popular." Grande was nominated for an Academy Award, a Golden Globe, a Critics' Choice Award, a British Academy Film Award, and a Screen Actors Guild Award.

WICKED

Wicked's soundtrack was released on November 22, 2024, the same day that the movie came out in theaters in the United States. It debuted at No. 2 on the _Billboard_ 200 with 139,000 units sold.[10] This includes physical and digital units and streaming. This set records, making it the highest debut for a soundtrack for a stage-to-film adaptation. Reviewing the soundtrack, Chris William of _Variety_ describes "No One Mourns the Wicked" as a song that showcased how Grande could make lines sound either comedic or operatic, a testimony to her voice work and classical training.

Whether she's on an arena stage, Broadway stage, television screen, or silver screen, Grande has proven to herself and the world that she has talent to spare. Part of Grande's success has been her willingness to stretch and try new things. Grande's fans are eagerly awaiting word of her upcoming projects.

ESSENTIAL FACTS

Full Name: Ariana Grande-Butera

Date of Birth: June 26, 1993

Place of Birth: Boca Raton, Florida

Parents: Joan Grande and Edward Butera

Education: North Broward Preparatory School

RISE TO STARDOM

- Ariana Grande performed in local theater as a child.
- She auditioned and got a part in the Broadway show *13* in 2008 when she was 15.
- Nickelodeon noticed her talent and invited her to audition for its new series *Victorious*.
- Her *Victorious* role as Cat Valentine built a fan base that helped her launch her musical career, beginning with her first album, *Yours Truly*.
- Social media and a strong fan following have helped drive Grande's success.

CAREER HIGHLIGHTS

- The single "Thank U, Next" was Grande's first No. 1 song.
- Her second album, *My Everything*, debuted at No. 1.
- In 2015, Grande went on the Honeymoon Tour, her first world tour.

- In 2019, Grande won her first Grammy for Best Pop Vocal Album for *Sweetener.*
- She returned to acting with her role as Galinda in *Wicked*.

MAJOR ALBUMS

- *Yours Truly* (2013)
- *My Everything* (2014)
- *Dangerous Woman* (2016)
- *Sweetener* (2018)
- *Thank U, Next* (2019)
- *Positions* (2020)
- *Eternal Sunshine* (2024)

QUOTE

"This music has always brought such comfort and now being able to spend time with it and be trusted with it is the privilege of a lifetime."

—Ariana Grande on performing in *Wicked*

GLOSSARY

a cappella
Sung without musical accompaniment.

cinematographer
A member of a film crew who oversees photography and camerawork.

contagious
When an illness can spread from one person to another.

crinoline
A stiffened petticoat that stands out to create a wide, bell-like skirt.

debut
The first time an actor, musician, or artist releases a product, such as an album; to release a single or album for the first time.

double entendre
A word or phrase that has two meanings, especially when one is sexual.

double standard
Rules or principles that are unfairly applied in different ways to different people or groups.

electronic dance music (EDM)
A style of music played at dance clubs that features electronic instruments such as synthesizers.

extended play (EP)
A musical recording that usually includes four to six songs.

gross
To earn income.

interpolation
Using portions of the melody from a previously recorded song.

maternal
Related to a mother's side of the family.

melisma
A group of notes sung to one syllable of a word.

post-traumatic stress disorder (PTSD)
A mental health condition brought on by a traumatic event.

public assistance
Government aid to people in need, such as vouchers to pay for housing or food.

run
A series of quickly sung notes.

scrim
In theater, a cloth, often behind the stage, used as a projection screen.

stenographer
A person who writes out what someone else says.

trap beat
A beat created with electronic or synth drums featuring specific drums such as snare or bass and high-hat cymbals.

understudy
A person who learns a theater role to act as a replacement if the main actor cannot play the part.

ADDITIONAL RESOURCES

SELECTED BIBLIOGRAPHY

Bote, Joshua, Jacqueline Reed, and Fengxue Zhang. "'Thank U' Text: Ariana Grande's Collaborators Break Down the Artist's Latest Album." *NPR*, 9 Feb. 2019, npr.org. Accessed 21 May 2025.

Mendez, Moises. "A Love Letter to Miley Cyrus' Backyard Sessions—and Her 5 Best Performances to Watch." *Time*, 10 Mar. 2023, time.com. Accessed 21 May 2025.

Zoladz, Lindsay. "Thank U, Next: How Ariana Grande and Drake Accelerated the Pop Music Life Cycle." *Ringer*, 5 Dec. 2018, theringer.com. Accessed 21 May 2025.

FURTHER READINGS

Calfee, Joel, Katie Connor, and Maura Johnston. *Ariana Grande: The Rise of a Dangerous Woman*. Hearst Home, 2025.

Edwards, Sue Bradford. *Making Music*. Abdo, 2025.

Popi, Alexis. *Cynthia Erivo*. Abdo, 2026.

ONLINE RESOURCES

To learn more about Ariana Grande, please visit **abdobooklinks.com** or scan this QR code. These links are routinely monitored and updated to provide the most current information available.

MORE INFORMATION

For more information on this subject, contact or visit the following organizations:

ACADEMY MUSEUM OF MOTION PICTURES

6067 Wilshire Blvd.
Los Angeles, CA 90036
academymuseum.org/en

The Academy Museum of Motion Pictures is the largest museum in the United States devoted to the art and science of moviemaking.

COSTUME INSTITUTE AT THE METROPOLITAN MUSEUM OF ART

1000 Fifth Ave.
New York, NY 10028
metmuseum.org/departments/the-costume-institute

The Costume Institute at the Metropolitan Museum of Art has a collection of more than 33,000 costumes and related objects. The Met Gala, which Ariana Grande attends each year, is a fundraiser to support the Institute.

GRAMMY MUSEUM

800 W. Olympic Blvd.
Los Angeles, CA 90015
grammymuseum.org

Music fans can listen to Grammy performances and also experiment with making their own music.

SOURCE NOTES

CHAPTER 1. LIVE!

1. Gabriel Lerman. "Ariana Grande: '"The Wizard of Oz" Has Been a Refuge for Many People Who Feel Lonely.'" *La Vanguardia*, 21 Nov. 2024, lavanguardia.com. Accessed 18 June 2025.

2. Josh Weiss. "How Many Oscars Did Wicked Win in 2025?" *NBC*, 3 Mar. 2025, nbc.com. Accessed 18 June 2025.

3. Melissa Ruggieri. "Oscars Musical Performance Review Including Ariana Grande and Cynthia Erivo." *USA Today*, 2 Mar. 2025, usatoday.com. Accessed 18 June 2025.

4. "Oscars 2025: Zoe Saldaña Wins Her First Academy Award." *YouTube*, uploaded by ABC News, 2 Mar. 2025, youtube.com. Accessed 18 June 2025.

5. "Oscars 2025."

6. Mary Varvaris. "Ariana Grande Locks In Collaboration with Mariah Carey." *Music*, 15 Feb. 2024, themusic.com.au. Accessed 18 June 2025.

7. "Ariana Grande Sails above Sorrow on 'Sweetener.'" *New York Times*, 29 Aug. 2018, nytimes.com. Accessed 18 June 2025.

CHAPTER 2. CHILDHOOD YEARS

1. Jason Lipschutz. "Gimme Five: Ariana Grande's Most Inspirational Female Singers." *Billboard*, 9 Oct. 2013, billboard.com. Accessed 18 June 2025.

2. Chris Murphy. "13 Was a Surprising Incubator for Talented Tots." *Vanity Fair*, 12 Aug. 2022, vanityfair.com. Accessed 18 June 2025.

3. "Ariana Grande." *Gayton Junior School*, n.d., gaytonj.derby.sch.uk. Accessed 18 June 2025.

4. Edward Wyatt. "First the Tween Heart, Now the Soul." *New York Times*, 25 Mar. 2010, nytimes.com. Accessed 18 June 2025.

5. Robert Seidman. "Nickelodeon Scores Second Biggest 'Kids' Choice Awards.'" *TV by the Numbers*, 29 Mar. 2010, tvbythenumbers.zap2it.com. Accessed 18 June 2025.

6. Andy Greene. "How Ariana Grande and Max Martin Made 'Problem' the Song of the Summer." *Rolling Stone*, 22 May 2014, rollingstone.com. Accessed 18 June 2025.

7. Stephanie Harper Dupont. "How Ariana Grande Relates to Cat Valentine on Nickelodeon." *Love Travel Beauty*, 4 Dec. 2024, lovetravelbeauty.com. Accessed 18 June 2025.

CHAPTER 3. BUILDING A MUSIC CAREER

1. Brenton Blanchet. "The 10 Best Ariana Grande Songs That Were Never Officially Released." *Billboard*, 18 Sept. 2019, billboard.com. Accessed 18 June 2025.

2. "Put Your Hearts Up." *RIAA*, 30 July 2014, riaa.com. Accessed 18 June 2025.

3. "The Way." *Song Facts*, n.d., songfacts.com. Accessed 18 June 2025.

4. "Ariana Grande Sued for Allegedly Copying Song Lyrics." *ABC News*, 12 Dec. 2013, abcnews.go.com. Accessed 18 June 2025.

5. Kyle Danis. "'Such a Breath of Fresh Air': Ariana Grande's 'Yours Truly' Collaborators Reflect on 10 Years of Her Debut Album." *Billboard*, 25 Aug. 2023, billboard.com. Accessed 18 June 2025.

6. KiMi Robinson. "Ariana Grande Shares Confessions about 'Yours Truly' Album, Including That 'Horrible' Cover." *USA Today*, 29 Aug. 2023, yahoo.com. Accessed 18 June 2025.

CHAPTER 4. AWARD WINNER

1. Louby McLoughlin. "Ariana Grande: 'I Look Back at Things I Wore Yesterday and Cringe.'" *Grazia*, 20 Aug. 2014, graziadaily.co.uk. Accessed 18 June 2025.

2. Keith Caulfield. "Ariana Grande's 'Problem' Set for Record Sales Debut." *Billboard*, 5 May 2014, billboard.com. Accessed 18 June 2025.

3. Jon O'Brien. "Ariana Grande's 'My Everything' Turns 10: Ranking All 12 Tracks a Decade Later." *Billboard*, 8 Aug. 2024, billboard.com. Accessed 18 June 2025.

4. Rob Sheffield. "My Everything." *Rolling Stone*, 26 Aug. 2014, rollingstone.com. Accessed 18 June 2025.

5. Sheffield, "My Everything."

6. Daniel Kreps. "The Who, Ariana Grande, and Dave Matthews Help Stand Up to Cancer." *Rolling Stone*, 6 Sept. 2014, rollingstone.com. Accessed 18 June 2025.

7. Timothy Finn. "Ariana Grande Delivers a Grand Spectacle at Independence Events Center (With Fan Reaction)." *Kansas City Star*, 26 Feb. 2015, kansascity.com. Accessed 18 June 2025.

8. "Ariana Grande Signs with Universal Music Publishing Group." *Billboard*, 1 June 2015, billboard.com. Accessed 18 June 2025.

CHAPTER 5. A LITTLE MOONLIGHT

1. Hannah Dailey. "Ariana Grande's 'Focus' Music Video Surpasses 1 Billion Views on YouTube." *Billboard*, 13 Mar. 2024, billboard.com. Accessed 18 June 2025.

2. Michael Cragg. "Ariana Grande: Dangerous Woman Review—A Refinement of Her Sound." *Guardian*, 22 May 2016, theguardian.com. Accessed 18 June 2025.

3. Christopher R. Weingarten. "Dangerous Woman: A Dangerous Pop Talent Searches for the Right Sound." *Rolling Stone*, 20 May 2016, rollingstone.com. Accessed 18 June 2025.

4. Kristin Corpus. "Ariana Grande Brings Dangerous Woman Tour to Madison Square Garden: Recap." *Billboard*, 1 Mar. 2017, billboard.com. Accessed 18 June 2025.

5. "Ariana Grande Lashes Out Against 'Double Standard and Misogyny.'" *ABC News*, 8 June 2015, abcnews.go.com. Accessed 18 June 2025.

6. "Survivors of 2017 Ariana Grande Concert Bombing Take Legal Action Against UK Intelligence Agency." *AP*, 14 Apr. 2024, apnews.com. Accessed 18 June 2025.

7. Daniel Gumble. "Ariana Grande One Love Manchester Show Draws TV Audience of 10.9 Million." *Music Week*, 5 June 2017, musicweek.com. Accessed 18 June 2025.

8. Korin Miller. "Ariana Grande Reveals She Has PTSD." *Women's Health*, 5 June 2018, womenshealthmag.com. Accessed 18 June 2025.

SOURCE NOTES

CHAPTER 6. *SWEETENER*

1. "Parkland Shooting: How the Attack Unfolded." *BBC*, 12 Oct. 2022, bbc.com. Accessed 18 June 2025.

2. Rania Aniftos. "Pharrell on Working with Ariana Grande on 'Sweetener.'" *Billboard*, 17 Aug. 2018, billboard.com. Accessed 18 June 2025.

3. Aniftos, "Pharrell on Working with Ariana Grande."

4. "No Tears Left to Cry." *Song Facts*, n.d., songfacts.com. Accessed 18 June 2025.

5. Sarah Hanlon. "A Deep Dive into Ariana Grande's Complete Dating History." *Knot*, 21 Nov. 2024, theknot.com. Accessed 18 June 2025.

6. Larry Fitzmaurice. "Ariana Grande's Sweetener Is a Sneakily Complex Pop Album." *Entertainment Weekly*, 20 Aug. 2018, ew.com. Accessed 18 June 2025.

7. Gwen Ihnat et al. "Ariana Grande and Mogwai Lead a Stellar Week in New Music." *AV Club*, 24 Aug. 2018, avclub.com. Accessed 18 June 2025.

8. Alexis Petridis. "Ariana Grande: Sweetener Review—Pop's Ponytailed Paragon Gets Weird." *Guardian*, 17 Aug. 2018, theguardian.com. Accessed 18 June 2025.

CHAPTER 7. HER OWN RULES

1. Charles Holmes. "Ariana Grande Wants to Release Music Like a Rapper." *Rolling Stone*, 5 Dec. 2018, rollingstone.com. Accessed 18 June 2025.

2. "Thank U, Next." *Song Facts*, n.d., songfacts.com. Accessed 18 June 2025.

3. "7 Rings." *Song Facts*, n.d., songfacts.com. Accessed 18 June 2025.

4. Andre Paine. "Ariana Grande Breaks Records with Thank U, Next's Chart Domination." *Music Week*, 15 Feb. 2019, musicweek.com. Accessed 18 June 2025.

5. Nicole Saunders. "Ariana Grande Is Reportedly Not Attending the Grammys." *Harper's Bazaar*, 7 Feb. 2019, harpersbazaar.com. Accessed 18 June 2025.

6. Joshua Bote et al. "'Thank U' Text." *NPR*, 9 Feb. 2019, npr.org. Accessed 18 June 2025.

7. Eric Frankenberg. "The Sweetener World Tour Finishes as Ariana Grande's Biggest Yet." *Billboard*, 23 Jan. 2020, billboard.com. Accessed 18 June 2025.

8. "The World's Highest Paid Celebrities." *Forbes*, n.d., forbes.com. Accessed 18 June 2025.

9. Ana Monroy Yglesias. "Ariana Grande Shines at Coachella." *Grammy Awards*, 15 Apr. 2019, grammy.com. Accessed 18 June 2025.

CHAPTER 8. *POSITIONS*

1. Kaitlin Reilly. "Ariana Grande and Taylor Swift Are Sending Money to Fans Who Lost Their Jobs Due to Coronavirus." *Refinery 29*, 27 Mar. 2020, refinery29.com. Accessed 18 June 2025.

2. Donald Judd. "Stacey Abrams and Andrew Yang Announce Push to Provide Direct Cash Payments to Families on Food Stamps." *CNN*, 21 Apr. 2020, edition.cnn.com. Accessed 18 June 2025.

CONTINUED. . .

3. Desiree Murphy. "Ariana Grande and Fiancé Dalton Gomez Send Gifts and Pizza to Children's Hospitals for the Holidays." *Entertainment Tonight*, 24 Dec. 2020, etonline.com. Accessed 18 June 2025.

4. Jack Irvin. "Ariana Grande Scrapped 'So Many Things' during Positions Album Cycle." *People*, 6 Nov. 2020, people.com. Accessed 18 June 2025.

5. Jaelani Turner-Williams. "Ariana Grande Says 'Positions' Reception Felt Like Getting 'Bullied.'" *Complex*, 6 Nov. 2024, complex.com. Accessed 18 June 2025.

CHAPTER 9. THE MET AND MORE

1. Mehera Bonner and Samantha Olson. "Ariana Grande's Nonna Gives Advice on When to Leave a Relationship in 'Eternal Sunshine.'" *Cosmopolitan*, 13 Mar. 2024, cosmopolitan.com. Accessed 18 June 2025.

2. Angeline Jane Bernabe. "Ariana Grande, Cynthia Erivo Perform Epic Duet at Met Gala." *ABC News*, 7 May 2024, abcnews.go.com. Accessed 18 June 2025.

3. "Ariana Grande Marks 10th Anniversary of 'My Everything' Album with Special Deluxe Edition." *GMA News Online*, 23 Aug. 2024, gmanetwork.com. Accessed 18 June 2025.

4. Christian Allaire. "'It's My Favorite Thing I've Ever Worn': Ariana Grande Talks Her 2024 Met Gala Looks." *Vogue*, 7 May 2024, vogue.com. Accessed 18 June 2025.

CHAPTER 10. THE BIG SCREEN

1. Bentley Maddox. "Ariana Grande Shares Dad's Emotional Reaction to Using His Last Name in Wicked Credits." *E News*, 12 Nov. 2024, eonline.com. Accessed 18 June 2025.

2. Mehera Bonner. "Kay, So Here's Why 'Wicked' Was Split Into Two Movies." *Cosmopolitan*, 24 Nov. 2024, cosmopolitan.com. Accessed 18 June 2025.

3. Annabel Rackham. "Ariana Grande Channeled Her Loss into Wicked Role." *BBC*, 20 Nov. 2024, bbc.com. Accessed 18 June 2025.

4. Rackham, "Ariana Grande Channeled Her Loss."

5. Rackham, "Ariana Grande Channeled Her Loss."

6. Grace Jidoun. "Why Ariana Grande and Cynthia Erivo's Live Singing on Wicked Had Everyone in Tears." *NBC*, 26 Nov. 2024, nbc.com. Accessed 18 June 2025.

7. Palmer Haasch. "13 'Wicked' Filming Secrets." *Business Insider*, 10 Dec. 2024, businessinsider.com. Accessed 18 June 2025.

8. Paul Grein. "'Wicked' Is Now the Top-Grossing Film Adaptation of a Broadway Musical: Full List." *Billboard*, 12 May 2025, billboard.com. Accessed 18 June 2025.

9. Peter Bradshaw. "Wicked Review." *Guardian*, 19 Nov. 2024, theguardian.com. Accessed 18 June 2025.

10. Keith Caulfield. "Kendrick Lamar's 'GNX' Debuts at No. 1 on Billboard 200." *Billboard*, 1 Dec. 2024, billboard.com. Accessed 18 June 2025.

INDEX

Academy Awards, 4, 99
Academy of Motion Picture Arts and Sciences, 4
Adele, 22
Alvarez, Ricky, 67
American Music Awards (AMAs), 31, 39–40, 69
Annie, 14
Ariana's Army, 22
Arianators, 22
Azalea, Iggy, 35, 38, 67

Backyard Sessions, The, 42
Barbie, 4
Baum, L. Frank, 6
Bennett, LeRoy, 71–72
Beyoncé, 60
Bieber, Justin, 28, 31, 52, 73, 76–77
Big Sean, 29, 34, 38, 42, 50, 67, 73
Billboard Music Awards, 72
Bodyguard, The, 17
Braun, Scooter, 28
British Academy Film Awards, 99
Butera, Edward, 12

Cardi B, 60–61
Carey, Mariah, 10, 11, 17, 22, 29, 68, 87, 90
Carrey, Jim, 34
Chu, Jon M., 94–95, 97
Crest Theater, 14
Critics' Choice Awards, 99
Cyrus, Miley, 18, 42, 52

Dangerous Woman, 46–48, 49–53, 60, 66
Davidson, Pete, 60, 67, 69
"Defying Gravity," 7–8, 97
Don't Look Up, 80

Erivo, Cynthia, 6–8, 89–90, 96–97, 99
Estefan, Gloria, 14
Eternal Sunshine, 86–88, 91
Etheridge, Melissa, 32

4 Non-Blondes, 24–25
Franklin, Aretha, 32

Garland, Judy, 4–6, 15
Gillies, Elizabeth, 18, 20
Glee, 18
Golden Globe Awards, 99
Gomez, Dalton, 77, 81, 84
Grammy Awards, 70
Grande, Frankie, 12
Grande, Joan, 12, 14, 15–17, 78, 92–94
Grande, Marjorie, 12, 88

Hairspray Live!, 49
Hannah Montana, 18
Heap, Imogen, 40, 52, 63
Houston, Whitney, 10, 17, 22, 34, 90

Iron Man 2, 6

Jessie J, 36, 40

K Bye for Now (SWT Live), 73
Kids' Choice Awards, 19
Kids Who Care, 17
Kotecha, Savan, 35, 59, 60

La La Land, 6
LaBelle, Patti, 32
lawsuits, 28, 59
Little Palm Family Theatre, 14, 17

Maguire, Gregory, 7
Manchester, England, 50–53, 57, 63, 69
March for Our Lives, 54
Martin, Max, 35, 38, 84
Met Gala, 88–90, 91
Mika, 26
Miller, Mac, 28–29, 50, 58, 67, 69, 71, 83
Minaj, Nicki, 36–37, 40, 59, 73
MTV Video Music Awards (VMAs), 57
My Everything, 37–40, 60, 90–91

North Broward Preparatory School, 14
NSYNC, 15, 73

Obama, Barack, 34
Obama, Michelle, 32
One Love Manchester, 52–53, 63, 66

People's Choice Awards, 32, 69
Perry, Katy, 40, 52
Perry, Linda, 24
Pine Crest School, 14
Positions, 77–80, 86–87
Project 100, 76
"Put Your Hearts Up," 24–26

Randolph, Da'Vine Joy, 8–9
Recording Industry Association of America (RIAA), 26, 37, 87
Republic Records, 22–24, 28, 30, 43

Saldaña, Zoe, 9
Salmanzadeh, Ilya, 35, 84
Sam & Cat, 27
Screen Actors Guild Awards, 99
Sivan, Troye, 58, 87
Slater, Ethan, 84
Snow White Christmas, A, 27
"Somewhere over the Rainbow," 6, 8, 53
Spears, Britney, 40
Squire, Matt, 24–25, 30
Stand Up to Cancer (SU2C), 39
Sweetener, 11, 54–63, 66, 69–73, 74
Swift, Taylor, 60
Swindle, 27

Thank U, Next, 66–69, 70, 71
13, 17–18
Tranter, Justin, 69, 70

Universal Music Group, 22, 87

Victorious, 18–21, 22–24, 27
Voice, The, 82

Weeknd, The, 39, 40, 82
Wicked (film), 6–7, 27, 89, 92, 94–99
Wicked (novel), 94
Wicked (play), 7, 27, 92–94
Williams, Pharrell, 54–56
Wizard of Oz, The, 4–7, 14
"Women of Soul: In Performance at the White House," 32, 34

Yours Truly, 24, 28–31, 35, 60, 82

Zedd, 36

ABOUT THE AUTHOR

SUE BRADFORD EDWARDS

Sue Bradford Edwards is a Missouri author who writes about culture and history, including the history of popular music. Her books about music and musicians include *Making Music*, *The Murders of Tupac and Biggie*, and *The Who*. Like Grande, she adores the music of Whitney Houston and Mariah Carey.